BLACK LIVES MATTER & MUSIC

Activist Encounters in Folklore and Ethnomusicology

David A. McDonald, editor

Edited by Fernando Orejuela
and Stephanie Shonekan

BLACK
LIVES
MATTER
&MUSIC

PROTEST, INTERVENTION, REFLECTION

Foreword by Portia K. Maultsby

Indiana University Press

This book is a publication of

Indiana University Press
Office of Scholarly Publishing
Herman B Wells Library 350
1320 East 10th Street
Bloomington, Indiana 47405 USA

iupress.indiana.edu

*Manufactured in the
United States of America*

*Library of Congress
Cataloging-in-Publication Data*

Names: Orejuela, Fernando, editor. |
    Shonekan, Stephanie, editor.
Title: Black Lives Matter and music : protest,
    intervention, reflection / edited by Fernando
    Orejuela and Stephanie Shonekan ;
    foreword by Portia K. Maultsby.
Description: Bloomington : Indiana University
    Press, 2018. | Series: Activist encounters
    in folklore and ethnomusicology
Identifiers: LCCN 2018021721 (print) |
    LCCN 2018025099 (ebook) | ISBN
    9780253038432 (e-book) | ISBN
    9780253038418 (hardback : alk. paper) |
    ISBN 9780253038425 (pbk. : alk. paper)
Subjects: LCSH: African Americans—
    Music—History and criticism. |
    Black lives matter movement.
Classification: LCC ML3556 (ebook)
    | LCC ML3556 .B57 2018 (print)
    | DDC 781.5/92—dc23
LC record available at https://
    lccn.loc.gov/2018021721

1 2 3 4 5   23 22 21 20 19 18

*This book is dedicated to our teachers and mentors,
especially the late Ronald R. Smith, who taught us to think
critically about race, life, art, and music.*

CONTENTS

FOREWORD

Portia K. Maultsby

FOR CENTURIES VARIOUS ETHNIC, CULTURAL, and social groups throughout the world have used music as a form of resistance against dictatorial rulers, oppressive governments, and capitalist structures. Folklorists, ethnomusicologists, African Americanists, cultural historians, and cultural sociologists have long recognized the power of music to empower people, to galvanize them into political action, and to sustain social movements. Their publications critique the role of music in labor movements (Fowke and Glazer 1973; Green et al. 2007), social movements (Eyerman and Jamison 1998; Roy 2010; Reagon 2017), and individual and group acts of defiance (Levine 1977; Maultsby 2015a, 2015b; Neal 2017), as well as its use to empower during and following conflict, violence, and war (Urla 2001; Hemetek 2006; McDonald 2009; O'Connell and Castelo-Branco 2010; Rogers 2012; Dave 2014). Since the seventeenth century, music has been central to the sociopolitical movements of black Americans, who continue to fight against all forms of institutional racism that impact negatively on black lives, especially in the areas of social justice, employment, housing, and education.

The Black Lives Matter movement is a contemporary expression of both pride and resistance, rooted in a tradition that began when Europeans used force to remove Africans from their homeland and place them into bondage. Chained together on the lower decks of ships and tightly packed much like sardines in a can, these black bodies endured all forms of inhumane treatment during the long voyage to the Americas. They were beaten, kicked around like animals, forced to lay in their own bodily waste, and required to dance to the beats of drums for exercise. Determined to retain their pride and dignity, on the ships and in the Americas, Africans engaged in acts of defiance by using the drum and coded song to communicate details to the masses.

Throughout the history of slavery in the United States, black male and female bodies suffered brutal beatings, dog maulings, hangings, and other savage acts of murder. In retaliation, the enslaved organized revolts and mapped out escape routes to freedom. Music played a central role in these acts of resistance. During the 1739 South Carolina Stono Rebellion, drums and loud horns became communication devices, signaling places to gather and times to strike. Following the enactment of laws by the colonies that forbade the playing of drums and other loud instruments, along with unsupervised gatherings, the enslaved turned to clandestine forms of communication. The use of the double entendre or coded texts in their spiritual songs, such as "Steal Away" and "Follow the Drinking Gourd," provided instructions for planned escapes to freedom. The enslaved also expressed defiance through song, proudly proclaiming, "Befo' I'd be a slave, I'd be buried in my grave, And go home to my Lord and be saved."

The rise of the Ku Klux Klan (KKK) following Reconstruction and the rigid Jim Crow laws led to open attacks on black bodies. Beatings and hangings became common forms of entertainment—violent acts of leisure—in rural white communities, with members of the KKK, sheriffs, and other law enforcement officers participating in these hideous crimes. Moreover, all-white juries ruled a "not guilty" verdict for any white perpetrator yet imposed a "guilty" verdict for any black person jailed on trumped-up charges, such as disrespecting a white man or woman. Everyday life proved challenging for black men, including those working on levee camps in Mississippi. Disregarding their economic value, Memphis Slims recalls that "them straw bosses would beat you dead. Mister Charlie say, 'Kill a nigger, hire another. But kill a mule you got to buy another.' You see they treated a mule better than a Negro back then in those camps" (Barlow 1989, 52).

The savage 1955 murder of Emmett Till, a fourteen-year-old boy from Chicago who had been visiting relatives in Mississippi and was accused of whistling at a white woman, continued one of many brutal acts of violence against black bodies that escalated and gave rise to the civil rights and Black Power movements. Local African American communities began organizing at the grassroots level and participating in various protest activities to force change in the oppressive conditions under which they lived. Music provided the source for inspiration and served as a tool for organizing and galvanizing communities into political action.

The Black Lives Matter movement continues the practice of using music as personal and group expressions to organize and peacefully protest racial injustices, including sanctioned police and civilian brutality against black bodies. Led by millennials in response to the unjustified murder of Tray-von Martin in 2013, followed by the killings of Mike Brown, Sandra Bland, and others in subsequent years, the scope of this movement is far-reaching. It encompasses social issues of environmental justice, criminal justice, and black political empowerment, highlighting themes of marginalization and black affirmation. Nevertheless, and overlapping the rise of the Black Lives Matter movement, we have witnessed increases in the membership of alt-right groups and the collaboration with the KKK, neo-Nazis, and neo-Confederates in public demonstrations. As they protested the removal of Confederate statues around the country, the hate rhetoric and violent activi-ties of these groups were on full display during the "Unite the Right" rally in Charlottesville, Virginia (August 12, 2017), which resulted in the killing of a counterprotester and injuring several others. President Donald Trump's laissez-faire attitude toward the expressions of white supremacy organiza-tions prompted the Black Lives Matter network to demand a ban on all Con-federate iconography and hate groups in the United States and to affirm, "We stand with the people of Charlottesville who are fighting for a world in which the inherent humanity of all people is honored" (Morrison 2017).

Against the backdrop of urban decay, community isolation, and limited financial resources, advocates of the Black Lives Matter movement use so-cial media and contemporary creative expressions—hip hop; R&B; go-go; techno; and the Houston, Texas, SLAB car culture—to expose and con-front these and other social injustices, and to inspire change through so-cial and political activism. Critics label Black Lives Matter as antipolice and anti-American, in the same way that they treated the Black Panthers Party for Self-Defense, a branch of the Black Power movement. Such views ig-nore centuries of racial animosities resulting from centuries of institutional racism and sanctioned violence inflicted on black bodies that produced adversarial relationships between law enforcement and African American communities (Harding 1981; Anderson 2016).

This history distinguishes the #BlackLivesMatter movement from the #AllLivesMatter response. White lives have always mattered, as evidenced by their privileged status, especially with regard to the criminal justice system and the ostensible "white-collar crime" category. Skin color frequently determines longer sentences for African Americans who have been convicted of the same crime committed by whites. Skin color also determines when drug use shifts from being a criminal offense to a treatable addiction. White privilege reigns supreme when judges grant the wealthy freedom or probationary sentencing for repugnant crimes (Muhammad 2010).

The contradiction of the #AllLivesMatter claim is most evident in the lack of racial diversity in the faculty of the nation's institutions of higher learning, where preference is given to a Eurocentric curriculum supported by a Eurocentric interpretation. Even more glaring is the lack of creative approaches to instruction that engages in nonthreatening conversations about race and ethnicity, which should begin in elementary school, and certainly by high school. How can we claim All Lives Matter when the majority of those lives are excluded from the educational curriculum? Music, especially hip hop and other contemporary forms, is a useful tool to explore race and a range of social issues. Such explorations potentially can contribute to a more nuanced and objective critique of the Black Lives Matter movement and also provide concrete evidence that All Lives Matter.

Black Lives Matter and Music: Protest, Intervention, Reflection expands on the vibrant roundtable discussions led by former students during the 2015 and 2016 conferences of the Society for Ethnomusicology and the American Folklore Society, respectively. The students' scholarly engagement with these disciplines extends from teaching and research to the social, cultural, and political activism that has gained traction through public ethnomusicology and applied folklore—those who apply their research to areas of public interest, contributing to what Jeff Titon calls "practice-informed theory" (1992, 315). Drawing from ethnographic research and personal encounters, the contributors illustrate how our work can add to the public awareness of the social, economic, political, scientific, and other forms of injustices in the society that spill over into institutions of higher learning and influence the curricula, pedagogical approaches, and treatment of minority students and faculty, as well as their responses to acts of resistance.

Black Lives Matter and Music foregrounds black music as a window into black life, thereby revealing the conditions that gave rise to and underscored the need for the Black Lives Matter movement. Moreover, it is a story about how black millennials demonstrate resilience and creativity as they challenge all forms of racial injustices, gender inequalities, and political systems that work against the empowerment of all black people—whether they reside in inner-city communities, middle-class suburbs, working-class neighborhoods, or rural towns. The chapters that follow range from personal experience to ethnographic studies to putting ethnomusicology to use and illustrating the role of music in acts of resistance that brought national attention to the Black Lives Matter movement.

WORKS CITED

Anderson, Carol. 2016. *White Rage: The Unspoken Truth of Our Unspoken Racial Divide.* New York: Bloomsbury.

Barlow, William. 1989. *Looking Up at Down: The Emergence of Blues Culture.* Philadelphia: Temple University Press.

Dave, Nomi. 2014. "The Politics of Silence: Music, Violence and Protest in Guinea." *Ethnomusicology* 58 (1): 1–29.

Eyerman, Ron, and Andrew Jamison. 1998. *Music and Social Movements: Mobilizing Traditions in the Twentieth Century.* Cambridge: Cambridge University Press.

Fisher, Miles Mark. 1990. *Negro Songs in the United States.* New York: Carol. Originally published in 1953.

Fowke, Edith, and Joe Glazer. 1973. *Songs of Work and Protest.* New York: Dover. Originally published in 1960 by the Labor Education Division of Roosevelt University.

Green, Archie, David Roediger, et al., eds. 2007. *The Big Red Songbook.* Chicago: Charles H. Kerr.

Harding, Vincent. *There Is a River: The Black Struggle for Freedom in America.* Orlando, FL: Harcourt Brace, 1981.

Hemetek, Ursula. 2006. "Applied Ethnomusicology in the Process of the Political Recognition of a Minority: A Case Study of the Austrian Roma." *Yearbook for Traditional Music* 38: 3–57.

Levine, Lawrence W. 1977. *Black Culture and Slave Consciousness: Afro-American Folk Thought from Slavery to Freedom.* New York: Oxford University Press.

Lovell, John. 1972. *Black Song: The Forge and the Flame.* New York: Macmillan.

Maultsby, Portia K. 2015a. "Funk." In *African American Music: An Introduction,* edited by Mellonee V. Burnim and Portia K. Maultsby, 301–319. New York: Routledge.

Maultsby, Portia K. 2015b. "Soul." In *African American Music: An Introduction*, edited by Mellonee V. Burnim and Portia K. Maultsby, 277–298. New York: Routledge.

McDonald, David A. 2009. "Poetics and the Performance of Violence in Israel/Palestine." *Ethnomusicology* 53 (1): 58–85.

Morrison, Aaron. "Black Lives Matter, Civil Rights Leaders Place Blame on Donald Trump for Charlottesville Violence." *Mic*, August 12, 2017, https://mic.com/articles/183687/black-lives-matter-civil-rights-leaders-place-blame-on-donald-trump-for-charlottesville-violence#.Cn4FRc42z.

Muhammad, Kahlil Gibran. 2010. *The Condemnation of Blackness: Race, Crime, and the Making of Modern Urban America*. Cambridge, MA: Harvard University Press.

Neal, Mark Anthony. 2017. "The Politics of Musical Creativity." In *Issues in African American Music: Power, Gender, Race Representation*, edited by Portia K. Maultsby and Mellonee V. Burnim, 368–380. New York: Routledge.

O'Connell, John Morgan, and Salwa el Shawan Castelo-Branco, eds. 2010. *Music and Conflict*. Urbana: University of Illinois Press.

Reagon, Bernice Johnson. 2017. "Music as an Agent of Social Change." In *Issues in African American Music: Power, Gender, Race Representation*, edited by Portia K. Maultsby and Mellonee V. Burnim, 343–367. New York: Routledge.

Rogers, Victoria. 2012. "John Blacking: Social and Political Activist." *Ethnomusicology* 56 (1): 63–85.

Roy, William G. 2010. *Reds, Whites, and Blues: Social Movements, Folk Music, and Race in the United States*. Princeton, NJ: Princeton University Press.

Titon, Jeff Todd. 1992. "Introduction: Music, the Public Interest, and the Practice of Ethnomusicology." *Ethnomusicology* 36 (3): 315–322.

Urla, Jacqueline. 2001. "We Are All Malcolm X: Negu Gorriak, Hip-Hop, and the Basque Political Imaginary." In *Global Noise: Rap and Hip-Hop outside the USA*, edited by Tony Mitchell, 171–193. Middletown, CT: Wesleyan University Press.

PORTIA K. MAULTSBY is Laura Boulton Professor Emerita of Ethnomusicology in the Department of Folklore and Ethnomusicology at Indiana University. She is editor with Mellonee V. Burnim of *African American Music: An Introduction*, and *Issues in African American Music: Power, Gender, Race, Representation*.

ACKNOWLEDGMENTS

SADLY, THE DEATH OF MICHAEL BROWN was not extraordinary, yet the ensuing events that emerged in Ferguson, Missouri, transformed observers of social injustices to take action nationwide. This transformational awareness resonated with the contributors to this volume, who were moved to hold a roundtable forum and then a panel on the aftermath of Ferguson, and these conversations ultimately led to this publication.

We would like to start by thanking the three women who put together the blueprint for a coalition of activists to come together in solidarity around the notion of social justice and racial equality: Alicia Garza, Opal Tometi, and Patrisse Cullors. Their initiative and the activist collectives who participate with the Black Lives Matter movement need to be acknowledged first and foremost. Their work has spurred so many necessary deliberations. We hope this book contributes to the discourse.

We also want to thank Janice Frisch, an acquisition editor at Indiana University Press, for approaching us and helping convert these orally delivered papers into a readable text format. It is also imperative to thank the other members of the press, such as Gary Dunham, Kate Schramm, and David Miller, for guiding us through the publication process. We would also like to thank and recognize our copyeditor Mary Jo Rhodes and indexer Eileen Allen.

Additionally, a special thanks to David A. McDonald for having faith in this project and including our edited volume in his book series. It is also important for us to acknowledge and thank the three anonymous reviewers who took great effort to critique our work and offer generous suggestions. The contributors would also like to thank those who have mentored us, read earlier drafts, and/or inspired us to complete this project: people like Gerald Donald of Drexciya, Dr. Lisa Brock, Dr. Richard Bauman, and, most importantly, Dr. Portia K. Maultsby. This book came about relatively quickly and, of course, this acknowledgment would not be completed without thanking our families—parents, partners, children, colleagues, and friends—who supported us over these past eleven months.

Finally, we remember with deep gratitude those citizens who were and continue to bear the brunt of racism and marginalization. You continue to inspire so many of us. To those who paid the ultimate price and to those who survived, too numerous to name, we honor you with this publication.

BLACK
LIVES
MATTER
&MUSIC

INTRODUCTION

Fernando Orejuela

"We gon' be alright! We gon' be alright!" More than a century of African American music-making, and the call for freedom, sustenance, and survival remains central. The hook from Kendrick Lamar's 2015 song, "Alright," was incorporated into a chant that reverberated at marches and demonstrations nationwide and was adopted as one of the most prevalent anthems of the Black Lives Matter movement. Reflecting on his influence on Kendrick Lamar's work, O.G. Ice Cube exclaimed, "I just feel like we're all a continuum of one thought, which is equality" (Goldman 2016, 53).[1] Lamar's hook echoes sonically a history of freedom songs created by African-descended people in the United States.

At protest rallies and marches, the "We gon' be alright!" chant is performed in the style and cadence and African American English vernacular delivered by Lamar's original recording. Drawing on the pioneering work of Bernice Johnson Reagon, the power of the chant comes from "the richness of Afro-American harmonic techniques and improvisation choral singing" (2001, 108). Johnson Reagon explains that the one-word lyric and sacred chant of "Amen" triggered subsequent refrains and codified lines understood by slaves in the performance of the spiritual. The musically simple chant engendered a new force when it shifted to the more literal "freedom" by student activists fighting for civil rights and social justice. "We gon' be alright!" is a re-versioning of that sonic tradition in the ongoing battle against oppression, disenfranchisement, inequality, exploitation, and death.

Lamar's song was released three years after Alicia Garza, a labor organizer for the National Domestic Worker's Alliance in Oakland, California, formed the nascent and largely dispersed coalition of activists whom we call Black Lives Matter. On July 13, 2013, the day George Zimmerman was found not guilty of second-degree murder and acquitted of manslaughter in the fatal shooting of Trayvon Martin, an unarmed black teenager walking home in his Sanford, Florida, neighborhood, Garza took to Facebook and wrote an open "love letter to black people." Dismayed by the response of some Americans, she wrote, "The sad part is, there is a section of America who is cheering and celebrating right now. . . . I continue to be surprised how little black lives matter. . . . Black people. I love you. I love us. Our lives matter." Along with Opal Tometi and Patrisse Cullors, the trio popularized the phrase as a hashtag on Twitter and Tumblr, sparking discussion about race and equality around the world. The hashtag then led to a networked movement. Disappointment and grief might have initiated the first responses, but the Black Lives Matter movement inaugurates a new era in the struggle for racial justice.

The idea for this book, *Black Lives Matter and Music: Protest, Intervention, Reflection,* grew out of several discussions with colleagues and a pair of academic conference presentations. In January 2015, my colleague Stephanie Shonekan approached me and other ethnomusicologists, Fredara Hadley, Eileen M. Hayes, Langston Collin Wilkins, and Denise Dalphond, to participate in a forum at the 2015 annual meeting for members of the Society for Ethnomusicology. We held a roundtable discussion titled "Black Music Matters: Taking Stock" to consider the threats and challenges to black music scenes as well as the strength of black music and its ability to serve as an expression of black life in the midst of the Black Lives Matter movement.

Since that moment, many other African Americans have died, many at the hands of the police, but the killing of Michael Brown of Ferguson, Missouri, on August 9, 2014, a significant tipping point, catapulted the Black Lives Matter movement into plain view on social media sites and news networks. At the same time, musicians started releasing songs in tandem with the movement's development. Songs like J. Cole's "Be Free" (2014), D'Angelo and the Vanguard's "The Charade" (2014), The Game's "Don't Shoot" (2014), Janelle Monáe's "Hell You Talmbout" (2015), Usher's

"Chains" (2015), Kendrick Lamar's "Alright" (2015), and others provided a thematic soundscape the panelists could analyze and critique—activist music flooding the airwaves and heralding a new period of activism for the second millennium.[2] However, a series of events at our colleague's university in particular made us reconsider our approach.

On November 3, 2015, Jonathan Butler, a University of Missouri graduate student, started his hunger strike in an effort to force the president of the university to resign for his lack of concern and inaction regarding the racial violence experienced by students of color on the Mizzou campus. This event coincided with the protests in Ferguson that were in collaboration with the Black Lives Matter movement. The students on campus took action. Some faculty took action. The Mizzou football team took action. On November 9, 2015, President Tim Wolfe announced his resignation and Butler ended his hunger strike.

Each of the panelists came to the conference with a different presentation than we had intended or had originally prepared. Analysis and critique of music text and sonic dimensions remain important to what we do, but we came to the event addressing other facets of the Black Lives Matter movement as they have affected our regions. We approached the topic locally, and personally. The conversation that ensued at the conference was energetic, uncomfortable, and very necessary. Lively discourse is good, but we remained unsatisfied. More trauma, injustices, and heartbreaks were yet to slow down. Given our training in ethnomusicology and folklore as well as the common concerns with common problems in folkloristics, ethnomusicology, and other disciplines in the social and cultural studies arena, we thought it was important to have a similar dialogue at the 2016 annual meeting of the American Folklore Society. We brought with us younger scholars, Langston Collin Wilkins and Alison Martin, who were closer in age to the activists mobilized at Black Lives Matter demonstrations. In the twelve months that passed between these two conferences, the tragic killings of unarmed black men and women continued at an alarming rate and in conjunction with the volume and intensity of the varied reactions and critiques of the American criminal justice system.

As a collective, we felt compelled to expand on the evolving narratives and discourses that continued without effective solutions sixty years after the civil rights movement. For *Black Lives Matter and Music*, we agreed to rework our talks with the goal to maintain some of the orality of the original forum and paper presentations in which we presented these ideas and to integrate them with more traditional scholarly writing. Meanwhile, it is incredibly important for us to keep the works accessible to a wide range of readers—participants and players, observers and respondents—who all are involved in, and affected by, the events of the last few years in particular. We are five scholars trained in ethnomusicology and folklore, who have been concerned with racial unrest in the United States and inspired by the Black Lives Matter movement that focuses on the physical, historical, and cultural value of black lives. Our aim for *Black Lives Matter and Music* is to facilitate a discussion about ideas and approaches important to applying critical, scholarly, experiential, and activist ethnomusicology in our work.

We come from a tradition that is unique in the discipline of ethnomusicology. All of us on both panels were trained at Indiana University in the only ethnomusicology program in the United States that resides in the College of Arts and Sciences and not in the School of Music. Furthermore, those of us that entered the program before 2000 had received our degrees from the Department of Folklore. The three younger contributors received their ethnomusicology degrees from the Department of Folklore and Ethnomusicology, so our work ebbs and flows between the two disciplines.

Ethnomusicology at Indiana University has its roots in the Department of Anthropology, with the arrival of George Herzog in 1948 and the founding of the Archives of Traditional Music. He was followed by George List (Folklore Institute) and Alan Merriam (Anthropology) (Archives of Traditional Music 2011). In 2000, the program became a full partner in the renamed Department of Folklore and Ethnomusicology and was reorganized into two separate disciplinary tracks. Institutionalizing ethnomusicology in the College of Arts and Sciences is important in terms of recognizing a separate category of research and a named degree concentration.

The contributors to this volume who began the program before 2000 were required to learn the canons of ethnomusicology and folklore in order to complete the masters or PhD degrees. The contributors to this volume who came after 2000 could choose to learn both canons. Some of us identify as both folklorist and ethnomusicologist. Some of us do not. All of us are affiliated with African American and African diasporic studies and we recognize the importance of tradition in our study of African American culture and the ways that the verbal arts, song, music, dance, narrative, and everyday-life activities are intersectionally connected to one another and the Africanisms that connect it to an African heritage.

Our engagement with race and ethnic critical studies is profoundly influenced by our experiences in this unique academic environment. My first encounter regarding resistance in academic writing in folklore came as a graduate student in my second semester reading Zora Neale Hurston's *Mules and Men* (1935). Hurston, a pioneering autoethnographer, and creative storyteller, tells us, "The white man is always trying to know into somebody else's business. All right, I'll set something outside the door of my mind for him to play with and handle. He can read my writing but he sho' can't read my mind. I'll put this play toy in his hand, and he will seize it and go away. Then I'll say my say and sing my song" (Hurston [1935] 1978, 5). There is a lot to unpack in just the first few pages of her ethnography, which addresses her experiential relationship with racism and appropriation in the academy.

There are scholars important to the two disciplines from which we come, including Portia K. Maultsby, William H. Wiggins, Gerald L. Davis, John Roberts, Mellonee Burnim, Gladys-Marie Fry, Ronald Smith, and Bernice Johnson Reagon (especially her work with Smithsonian Folklife). Their work remains revelatory to students studying expressive culture and its relation to civil rights.[3] These writers came to the field of folklore and ethnomusicology with an activist's mission, developed from their experiences growing up during the Jim Crow era, the civil rights movement, and through their involvement with civil rights and Black Power. Together, their scholarship and special projects opened doors that became wide open with articles on African influences and retentions, slave spirituals and the idea of freedom, the evolution of African American popular music, and the history and contributions of African-descended people in the United States.

There has been a fairly long tradition of activism in folklore studies, most often realized in the areas of applied folklore and applied ethnomusicology, and this volume aims to dialogue with and be a part of this work and discussion. Spanning back across the two disciplines, we can see some of the roots of activist scholarship in Benjamin A. Botkin's work with the Library of Congress in the 1930s and 1940s, which helped to found the movement toward applied folklore. Hand-in-hand with this movement toward activism came pushback against the politicization of our roles as scholars and the communities we study. In folklore this resistance came mostly from the old guard as the American Folklore Society discussed how to recognize and support applied folklore within its own structure during the Middle Atlantic Conference on Folk Culture held from May 22–23, 1971. The debates, cosponsored by the Pennsylvania Folklore Society, the Committee on Applied Folklore of the American Folklore Society, and Point Park College, brought forth a number of opinions, with Richard Bauman and Richard Dorson supplying two of the more interesting opposing perspectives that were subsequently printed in the journal *Folklore Forum* (Bauman 1971; Dorson 1971). Building out of this early 1970s debate has been a greater discussion of how to effectively work as both scholars and activists through foundational publications from scholars such as Jeff Todd Titon, Michael Owen Jones, Debra Kodish, and many others.[4]

Realizing that our work is not separated from who we are—as African Americans, African, or allies—we find ourselves at a critical nexus of scholarship and activism. Activism comes in different forms. Rap and R&B artists had already begun to signify on the crisis and social movement themselves. As scholars, our work has the potential to reach different audiences by taking the discourse beyond the academic spaces of music appreciation, audiophilia, and the description of "political" music toward spaces that impact actionable changes in favor of racial equality in the United States. The contributors to this volume have been deeply affected by the events that happen to the communities we study, and we have a certain amount of privilege to advocate for social and political change for minority communities. We feel it is our responsibility to connect with people inside and outside the academy.

This brief intellectual history of ethnomusicology and folklore situates this text, *Black Lives Matter and Music*, within a tradition of innovation, resistance, discovery, and endeavors to push forth new perspectives for critical activism and scholarly intervention. At certain points in that intellectual history, some of our predecessors' findings could be identified as revolutionary. While their work remains important to current folklorists and ethnomusicologists, it is the intention of the contributors of *Black Lives Matter and Music* to move in a direction that highlights the experiential quests related to our ethnographic and autoethnographic projects with purposeful outcomes or exploratory possibilities for ethnomusicological and folkloristic activism in the teaching of and public practice with protest identities. That is, methods, theory, and actions to further social awareness that will add to and go beyond aestheticizing culture, the classification of songs and artifacts, structural analyses, performative stylistics, and regional differentiation of a musical art community descending from Africa. The Black Lives Matter movement is not the civil rights movement. It is something else. It is a motivating, dynamic movement still developing in the second millennium, mobilizing similar programs, organizations, and interested allies protesting racial injustice today to work together.

Because black music and vernacular forms frame much of *Black Lives Matter and Music*, we strive to bring to light not just the unfinished narratives that are yet to be realized but rather the recurring or revitalized narratives that have been pronounced in epochs since enslavement, Jim Crow, the civil rights movement, the Black Power movement, and the Los Angeles uprising of 1992. From Trayvon to Mike Brown to Sandra Bland to Freddie Gray to Alton Sterling to Philando Castile to Stephon Clark, these are just a few names that have become shorthand points of reference, flash points created from grand juries' nonindictment for the killing of black men and women in the early years of this new millennium.

In this book, we try to capture concisely the interweaving of our experiences, situations, and motivations as scholars trying to do the work on campus, in the classroom, in the field, or in the neighborhoods. As a collective, we present various forms of protest, solidarity, and solace that range from civilian action to institutional inaction that produce or uphold the tragic conditions that mark this current juncture of American history. In *Black Lives Matter and Music*, each author details a particular concern to help facilitate productive dialogue that can be generated in the undergraduate as well as the graduate classroom: a case of student protests on a college campus; a case of ethnomusicological and folkloristic pedagogies, campus life, and insensitive university administrations; a case of the social importance ascribed to the carnivalesque parades of a local, vernacular car culture; and two cases of musicians and disc jockeys affirming black life and resisting institutional forces through unique music scenes in Detroit and Washington, DC, respectively. Geographic location is essential, and each contributor focuses on a specific city that corresponds to the national scope of the movement and regional variation concerning these matters.

The chapters are organized in the following way:

Stephanie Shonekan presents a scholarly reaction to her experience at the University of Missouri when students were driven to action by the inaction of campus administration to address an uncomfortable and racist environment on campus and in town. Their stories and songs marked significant moments during the black student movement at the University of Missouri. She focuses on the climate of the campus one year later by reflecting on the music of the movement, the story behind a uniquely, unprecedented program and composition by the School of Music's choir, and the collaborative music project that faculty and students had created to help inspire conversations about race and identity on campus with respect to the Black Lives Matter movement.

Fernando Orejuela begins his chapter addressing the passively hostile, teaching environment of a big state university campus in the rural Midwest and the practice of teaching about racial inequality through hip hop musical communities while simultaneously bringing to light the experiences of teaching in the midst of racial unrest in the United States. His chapter asks two questions: What role do we have as scholars to resist the educational institution's assertions supporting a Eurocentric collegiate universe? What can ethnomusicological and folkloristic pedagogies centered on art, resistance, racial violence, microaggressions, and their aftermath look like? His project attempts to take a next step, *après* critique, by engaging and utilizing activist pedagogy. Orejuela presents a response to the pros and cons of his own teaching assignment to understand better interdiscursivity in the educational setting.

In the following chapter, Langston Collin Wilkins draws on his ethnographic research period to discuss the 2013 Houston SLAB Parade as a case study to argue for increased scholarly attention to and public programming around contemporary African American folklife. As a collaborative event organized by members of the community and a resident scholar, the first-ever Houston SLAB Parade and Family Festival was established to celebrate a long-running, African American custom car tradition in Houston, Texas. Wilkins discusses aspects of his fieldwork in the SLAB community, how local institutions partnered with the SLAB community to organize the parade, and why such investments into contemporary African American folklife can help reshape the social narrative of a place and help build toward a more culturally pluralistic future.

Drawing on the core ideals of Black Lives Matter as a framework, Alison Martin addresses narratives told within local, black musical spaces, and considers how these stories engage with the ideas of solidarity and resistance that are central to the Black Lives Matter movement. Specifically, Martin uses her ethnographic research project on go-go music and gentrification in Washington, DC, to engage with Black Lives Matter and demonstrate how go-go musicians affirm black life and resist institutional forces within live performance. Furthermore, exploring the negotiation between resistance and affirmation within black musical space provides a key site for activism and scholarship in both folklore and ethnomusicology.

Finally, in Denise Dalphond's chapter, the author argues that Detroit's techno and house music scene built on a rebellious legacy of local, black music-making, and that black electronic music culture in Detroit provides soundscapes and physical frameworks for real social change by insulating and isolating its musical artists and activists. According to her ethnographic research, Detroiters' entrepreneurial spirit built each element of music industry production and circulation locally, including vinyl record production and distribution. Dalphond argues that this spirit and local mythologies attached to the scene make the majority-black city of Detroit truly self-sufficient and ripe for major social and cultural change with connections to the Black Lives Matter movement.

Black Lives Matter and Music aims to highlight the distinctions between the ways politically and socially conscious individuals utilize black music culture and folkways by way of protest movements, music performances, material culture festivities, or pedagogy. We all attempt to contrast ways that black music scenes might be thought to organically create the context for political and cross-cultural engagement. We argue that the power of black musical vernacular culture—not simply as artistic forms—is best realized within the context of structured political and civic activities.

Writing a book like *Black Lives Matter and Music* took a toll on each of us to complete. It has been and continues to be difficult to separate our emotions from the topics we write about. I began writing the introduction on the day a St. Anthony police officer, Jeronimo Yanez, was acquitted in the shooting death of Philando Castile, a motorist who was pulled over for a broken taillight and then shot seven times in front of his fiancé and her four-year-old daughter. It was yet another death of an African American and a testimony to the failure of our judicial system in these matters. The City of St. Anthony agrees. On the same day of the acquittal, the city released a statement admitting that the public would "be best served if Officer Yanez is no longer a police officer in our city," committing "to help him transition to another career other than being a St. Anthony officer" (Chavey 2017).

I finished the draft of this introduction while watching a news report on the attempts of Camden, New Jersey, police officers to change the direction and attitude about policing their areas—from a warrior mentality to a guardian perspective—incorporating members of the community to join the police force in an effort to build trust where there has historically been none (Sreenivasan 2017). Optimism is necessary for healing to happen, even with the anticipation of more death and injustices at the back of our collective minds. I have hope and am inspired by the words of India Arie: "Every time I turn on the T.V. [*There's hope*] / Somebody's acting crazy [*There's hope*] / If you let it, it'll drive you crazy [*There's hope*] / But I'm takin' back my power today [*There's hope*]."

In the late 1970s, Audre Lorde offered advice that resonates well in our country's current state: "Difference must be not merely tolerated, but seen as a fund of necessary polarities between which our creativity can spark like a dialectic. Only then does the necessity for interdependency become unthreatening. Only within that interdependency of different strengths, acknowledged and equal, can the power to seek new ways to being in the world generate, as well as the courage and sustenance to act where there are no charters" ([1984] 1996, 111).

Scholars and musicians have aided in terms of decolonizing our listening, vision, and thinking; the Black Lives Matter movement, its subsidiary coalitions, and its activists ask us to countercolonize the establishment. I close our introduction in the same way I began: with song. "Now let's get in formation . . . best revenge is your paper."

Notes

1. "O.G." stands for "original gangster" or "original gangsta." This slang term is frequently used among hip hop aficionados to describe a revered veteran of the rap music scene.

2. And joined by pop rap, gangsta rap, and conscious rap artists: Diddy, Rick Ross, 2 Chainz, Fabolous, Wale, DJ Khaled, Swizz Beatz, Yo Gotti, Curren$y, Problem, King Pharaoh, Tyrese, Ginuwine, and Tank.

3. These scholars came into the disciplines of folklore and ethnomusicology at a time when conservative folklorists and musicologists were holding on to the frameworks perpetuated by cultural evolutionists, dismissing black people's art or sophistication in terms of music-making. Regarding folk narrative and folklife, see Gladys-Marie Fry's seminal book *Night Riders in Black Folk History* (1975) as well as her 1990 work on slave quilts; Gerald L. Davis's *I Got the Word in Me and I Can Sing It, You Know: A Study of the Performed African-American Sermon* (1987); and John Roberts's *From Trickster to Badman: The Black Folk Hero in Slavery and Freedom* (1990). Also important to the field are William H. Wiggins's work on celebrations, such as Juneteenth, and his book *O Freedom: Afro-American Emancipation Celebrations* (1987), and Bernice Johnson Reagon's work for the Smithsonian, such as her 1970 Folkways festival program *Black Music through the Languages of the New World* as well as her performances on Folkway albums from the 1960s to her work with Sweet Honey in the Rock. For works on defining the black musical aesthetic framing the boundaries of music performances, see Portia K. Maultsby's "Influences and Retentions of West African Musical Concepts in US Black Music" (1979) and "Soul Music: Its Sociological and Political Significance in American Popular Culture"; Ronald R. Smith's "Afro-American Folk Music" (1983); and Mellonee Burnim's "Culture Bearer and Tradition Bearer: An Ethnomusicologist's Research on Gospel Music" *(1985). In terms of educational resources, see Maultsby's* "The Evolution of African American Music" ([1988] 2009), a chart that illustrates the development of African American music from African origins to popular music of the 2000s, and her 1985 article, "The Role of Scholars in Creating Space and Validity for On-Going Changes in Black American Culture." Together, Burnim and Maultsby provide students and scholars with two seminal reads on black music studies *African American Music: An Introduction* (2015) and *Issues in African American Music: Power, Gender, Race, Representation (2017)*.

4. Other important contributions in academic writing include Michael Owen Jones's edited volume, *Putting Folklore to Use* (1994); the special issue of the *Journal of the Folklore Institute Journal of Folklore Research* 35, no. 3 (Sep.–Dec. 1998)—especially the articles by Jessica M. Payne and David Shuldiner—or, more currently, Debra Kodish's article from 2011. For ethnomusicology, Jeff Todd Titon's special issue on music and the public interest that he edited for the journal *Ethnomusicology* in 1992 paved the way for John Fenn to edit a special issue on applied folklore and ethnomusicology for the journal *Folklore Forum* in 2003, and Klisala Harrison, Elizabeth Mackinlay, and Svanibor Pettan produced their ambitious edited volume, *Applied Ethnomusicology:*

Historical and Contemporary Approaches, in 2010. Anchored in definitions and practices employed by ethnomusicologists all over the world, the contributors discuss a variety of topics that affect ethnomusicologists in the field and the classroom, such as social justice and music, pedagogies and educational reform, ethics in ethnomusicology, medical ethnomusicology, advocacy, and our positionality.

WORKS CITED

Archives of Traditional Music. 2011. "History." Trustees of Indiana University. http://www.indiana.edu/~libarchm/

Bauman, Richard. 1971. "Proposal for a Center of Applied Folklore." *Folklore Forum Bibliographic and Special Series: Papers on Applied Folklore* 8: 1–5. http://hdl.handle.net/2022/2633

Burnim, Mellonee. 1985. "Culture Bearer and Tradition Bearer: An Ethnomusicologist's Research on Gospel Music." *Ethnomusicology* 29 (3): 432–447.

Burnim, Mellonee V., and Portia K. Maultsby, eds. 2015. *African American Music: An Introduction.* New York: Routledge.

Chavey, Sarah M. 2017. "Yanez Will Not Return to Work for St. Anthony Police." *Twin Cities Pioneer Press,* June 16, 2017. http://www.twincities.com/2017/06/16/yanez-will-not-return-to-work-for-st-anthony-police/

Davis, Gerald L. 1987. *I Got the Word in Me and I Can Sing It, You Know: A Study of the Performed African-American Sermon.* Philadelphia: University of Pennsylvania Press.

Department of Folklore and Ethnomusicology. "History." Trustees of Indiana University. Last Updated, 05/29/12. http://www.indiana.edu/~folklore/ethno_about.shtml

Dorson, Richard M. 1971. "Applied Folklore." *Folklore Forum: Bibliographic and Special Series: Papers on Applied Folklore* 8: 40–42. http://hdl.handle.net/2022/2641

Fenn, John, ed. 2003. *Folklore Forum: Special Issue on Applied Folklore and Ethnomusicology* 34 (1/2).

Fry, Gladys-Marie. 1975. *Night Riders in Black Folk History.* Knoxville: University of Tennessee Press.

———. 1990. *Stitched from the Soul: Slave Quilts from the Ante-Bellum South.* New York: Dutton Studio Books (in association with the Museum of American Folk Art).

Garza, Alicia. 2014. "A Herstory of the #BlackLivesMatter Movement." *The Feminist Wire,* October 7. Accessed March 2, 2017. http://www.thefeministwire.com/2014/10/blacklivesmatter-2/.

Goldman, Justin. 2016. "Of Ice Cube: The Hemi Q&A." *Hemespheres Magazine.* April: 52–55.

Harrison, Klisala, Elizabeth Mackinlay, and Svanibor Pettan, eds. 2010. *Applied Ethnomusicology: Historical and Contemporary Approaches.* Cambridge: Cambridge University Press.

Hurston, Zora Neale. (1935) 1978. *Mules and Men.* Bloomington: Indiana University Presss.

Jones, Michael Owen, ed. 1994. *Putting Folklore to Use*. Lexington: University of Kentucky Press.

Kodish, Debora. 2011. "Envisioning Folklore Activism." *Journal of American Folklore* 124 (491): 31–60.

Lorde, Audre. (1984) 1996. "The Master's Tools Will Never Dismantle the Master's House." In *Sister Outsider: Essays & Speeches*. Freedom, CA: Crossing Press.

Maultsby, Portia K. 1979. "Influences and Retentions of West African Musical Concepts in U.S. Black Music." *Western Journal of Black Studies* 3 (Fall 1979): 197–215.

———. 1983. "Soul Music: Its Sociological and Political Significance in American Popular Culture." *Journal of Popular Culture* 17 (2): 51–60.

———. 1985. "The Role of Scholars in Creating Space and Validity for On-Going Changes in Black American Culture." In *Black American Culture and Scholarship: Contemporary Issues*, edited by Bernice Johnson Reagon, 9–23. Washington, DC: Smithsonian Institution.

———. (1988) 2009. "The Evolution of African American Music." In *The Political Calypso: A Sociolinguistic Process of Conflict Transformation*, edited by Everard M. Philips, 12–14. Port of Spain, Trinidad: Personal Power Unlimited, 2009.

Maultsby, Portia K. and Mellonee V. Burnim, eds. 2017. *Issues in African American Music: Power, Gender, Race, Representation*. New York: Routledge

Reagon, Bernice Johnson. 2001. *If You Don't Go, Don't Hinder Me: The African American Sacred Song Tradition*. Abraham Lincoln Lecture Series. Lincoln: University of Nebraska Press.

Roberts, John. 1990. *From Trickster to Badman: The Black Folk Hero in Slavery and Freedom*. Philadelphia: University of Pennsylvania Press

Smith, Ronald R. 1983. "Afro-American Folk Music." In *Handbook of American Folklore*, edited by Richard M. Dorson, 24–31. Bloomington: Indiana University Press.

Sreenivasan, Hari. 2017. "What Happened When Camden Started Rethinking Policing to Build Trust." *PBS NewsHour*, June 30, 2017. http://www.pbs.org/newshour/bb/happened-camden-started-rethinking-policing-build-trust/.

Titon, Jeff Todd, ed. 1992. *Ethnomusicology: Special Issue: Music and the Public Interest*. 36 (3).

Wiggins, William H., Jr. 1987. *O Freedom: Afro-American Emancipation Celebrations*. Knoxville: University of Tennessee Press.

———. 2010. "Juneteenth: A Red Spot Day on the Texas Calendar." In *Juneteenth Texas: Essays in African-American: Essays in African-American Folklore*, edited by Francis Edward Abernethy, Patrick B. Mullen, and Alan B. Govenar, 237–254. Publications of the Texas Folklore Society. Denton: University of North Texas Press.

FERNANDO OREJUELA is Senior Lecturer and Director of Undergraduate Studies in the Department of Folklore and Ethnomusicology at Indiana University. He is the author of *Rap Music and Hip Hop Culture*.

ONE

BLACK MIZZOU: MUSIC AND STORIES ONE YEAR LATER

Stephanie Shonekan

AN OCTOBER EVENING IN THE fall of 2016 felt like déjà vu. The multipur-
pose room of the Gaines-Oldham Black Culture Center at the University
of Missouri (Mizzou) was packed. The mood was somber. Black student
leaders had called an emergency town hall meeting. The night before, some
black students had been called the N-word and misogynistic expletives by
a group of white students standing outside the entrance to their fraternity
house. It felt like déjà vu because almost exactly one year earlier, Payton
Head, the student body president, who happens to be African American, as
well as a group of students of the Legion of Black Collegians had been called
the N-word all in the span of one week. Given the power of language and
the value of semiotics, it was no surprise that the one word triggered a series of events—a hunger strike, a series of protests and marches, the Mizzou
football players' boycott, two powerful administrators stepping down, and
a stream of threats toward the lives of black folks by way of a social network
app, Yik Yak. To say that this was a major crisis would be an understatement
as the university served as the epicenter for protests on many campuses
across the country.

The question on all our minds at the town hall meeting that October evening was whether anything had changed. Since the events of the previous
year, the university had worked hard to push for change—working with a
widening circle of institutional and individual allies, creating a diversity

14

program for incoming freshmen, installing diversity requirements across colleges and schools, and hosting a stream of speakers like the author and legal expert Bryan Stevenson (whose work *Just Mercy: A Story of Justice and Redemption* was published in 2014); the activist Diane Nash, who had marched with King in Selma; and many others. These new responses to a continuing practice of "old-school" racism were a reminder that we had simply scratched the surface of a big and wide system of oppression that has been built over hundreds of years. In other words, what happened on the Mizzou campus was a new episode in a continuum of racism that has been evolving since slavery, and in response, every generation has produced a mode of black liberation.

I contend that at the heart of every black liberation movement in the United States, there is the accompanying sound of black music that serves as a soundtrack for each wave of the movement. During the civil rights movement, as King and Lewis were engaged in a 1960s precursor to the Black Lives Matter movement, Aretha Franklin, Nina Simone, and the Staple Singers performed songs that spoke directly to the work of the activists. Music accompanied the marches and sit-ins. Examining the impact of soul music in the 1960s, the ethnomusicologist Portia Maultsby reveals that "performers of soul music, in communicating the philosophy of the Black Power Movement, promoted the black pride or self-awareness concept" (1989, 168). This notion has reappeared in the evolution of the music through the decades. This chapter acknowledges the link between black struggle and black music by examining the multiple ways that music was involved during and after the Mizzou movement. Like all the other movements that have been instigated by black folks around the world over the years, the movement on Mizzou's campus was suffused with music on every level and in every space.

As a scholar of black studies and ethnomusicology on the Mizzou campus, who had access to the students and their movement, I found myself considering the ways in which music featured for the collective, for individuals, and for the institution. I was interested in song choices for different individuals and for unique situations. Soul music and gospel music dominated the 1960s movement because those were the genres that had emerged at that time from an amalgamation of sacred and secular African American oral traditions. In the 2000s, that music has evolved to new genres rooted in the same common foundations. Thus, the music that serves this generation is new black music, and new black civil rights music. Like other activists before them, these students turned to the music of their generation for inspiration, motivation, and spiritual upliftment.

THE CONTEXT/THE MOVEMENT

In November 2015, a group of University of Missouri students led a powerful movement that shook the very foundations of the university. This movement of young black student activists finally grew tired of the racist environment in which they had to study. They spoke up and stood up with the ultimate goal of overturning the status quo. The product of that movement resulted in the resignations of the president and chancellor, an investigation of the curriculum, the establishment of unprecedented coalitions and caucuses, and the exposure of both openly practicing racists and passive racism in the form of microaggressions.

The roots of Mizzou's activism had begun a long time ago in the 1930s and 1940s when black students were not allowed to enroll on campus, to the 2010s, when, for example, cotton balls were strewn on the lawn outside the Gaines-Oldham Black Culture Center.[1] The former example was a consequence of institutionalized racism and Jim Crow in action; and the latter was an action by a few modern-day white students who were intent on sending a message to black students that they were nothing but cotton pickers, a clear reference to the days of slavery. From the 1930s to the present, the scrutiny of student activists was focused not only on the perpetrators of racist acts but also on the ways in which the administration reacted to these acts. In the case of the cotton balls, the administration chose to acknowledge this as littering and not as a racist occurrence (Heavin 2010). This inaction sent a clear message to the entire student body that the administration was unwilling to engage with the very troubling pattern of racism.

Such scrutiny was resurrected after the murder of Trayvon Martin in 2012, and it came to a head in the spring of 2015, when black students once again challenged the administration's silence after the murder of Mike Brown in August 2014 just down the road in Ferguson. Wesley Lowery asserts that "from Ferguson to Mizzou, it was fitting that Missouri played such a crucial role in the nation's reckoning with race and justice" (2016, 214).

Some students began to march peacefully, led by a group called MU for Mike Brown. Another group called Wage Peace led a silent burial procession across campus, holding make-shift coffins symbolizing the young black lives that had been murdered by police and other perpetrators. By this time, the Black Lives Matter movement had become the umbrella under which all these actions were taking place. Keeanga-Yamahtta Taylor asks, "Is it any wonder that a new movement has taken Black Lives Matter as its slogan when it is so clear that for the police, Black lives do not matter at all?" (2016, 3).

In the fall of 2015, the administration again turned a blind eye and deaf ear to reports of multiple macro- and microaggressions on campus: for instance, the school body president Payton Head and many others were called "nigger" while walking on campus. Reflecting on the viscerally hateful articulation of this deliberate version of the N-word, Head issued a passionate response by way of a Facebook post, which went viral and captured national attention. In response to these new occurrences, a graduate student named Danielle Walker started a campaign called RacismLivesHere. I watched as a small group became bigger, publicly taking over space in the student center and in the administrative building to raise awareness about the trauma that black students and other marginalized groups had been experiencing, and about the ways in which this racist environment obstructs the educational process for them, which white students do not have to contend with.

This call was carried forward into November 2015, when a group of eleven committed students called ConcernedStudent1950 (CS1950), in honor of the first year a black student was admitted to the university, began to carefully organize peaceful action, vibrant protests, and silent marches. Finally, during the homecoming parade, they blocked the car carrying the president of the University of Missouri system, Tim Wolfe. Their intention was to communicate to him the gravity of the situation. When he refused to engage in a conversation with the students, with his car actually nudging forward into the group, members of the wider Columbia community began to taunt the students. The police also stepped in to "protect" the president. As a result of this traumatic experience, Jonathan Butler, a graduate student, embarked on a hunger strike, insisting on the resignation of the president. This inspired the black football players to stop playing or practicing until conditions had been met to allow Butler to end his hunger strike.

When President Wolfe exposed his misunderstanding or miseducation regarding the meaning of systemic racism, the calls for his resignation grew stronger. It was unconscionable, the students and their allies insisted, for the president of a research, land-grant university to blame systemic racism on the very victims of the oppressive historical system. Joined by hundreds of mostly black students, CS1950 continued to march, hold sit-ins and die-ins, and set up camp in front of the administration building. They would not move, they said, until Jonathan Butler ate; the football players, backed by their coach, Gary Pinkel, would not play or practice until then; and Butler was adamant that he would not eat until the president resigned. Along with other colleagues, I supported from the sidelines, observing the atmosphere grow tense, as the line between revolution and rebellion became taut. A widening group of faculty and staff began to collect food and resources to feed the students who had joined the camp in the cold fall season. It is widely speculated that the shift came when the administration and the board calculated the millions of dollars at stake if the football players did not play in an upcoming Southeastern Conference game.

This social movement was also a sonorously musical movement. I began to notice the brilliant strains of black music permeating the students' activism. Even though, on a national level, the season was rife with frustrations about the appropriation of black music—with white artists like Iggy Azalea, Adele, Macklemore, and Demi Lovato gaining attention for their co-opting of black musical styles—this position of black music as a significant player in the movement reminded me of the real power of the music as an integral part of black life. While its commercial impact (for black people) seems to be receding, its cultural significance is as powerful as ever, just as scholars from Samuel Floyd, to Amiri Baraka, to Portia Mautlsby have maintained. At Mizzou, music certainly appeared to be a soundtrack for both the collective and the individuals.

THE COLLECTIVE: MUSIC OF THE MOVEMENT

One of the major lessons for me as I watched the events unfold in the fall of 2015 was that theory was becoming reality in the sense that, as a Nigerian-Trinidadian woman born on the other side of the globe in the year Martin Luther King Jr. was assassinated, I had only ever read about the ways in which socially conscious songs featured in the civil rights movement of the 1950s and 1960s. In his book *Sweet Soul Music*, Peter Guralnick traces the evolution of civil rights songs and explains, "Once [soul music] emerged from the underground, it accompanied the Civil Rights Movement almost step by step, its success directly reflecting the giant strides that integration was making" (1986, 2). The Mizzou movement provided a portal into the past, as students organized and marched, galvanized by the songs they sang in unison. New civil rights songs were chanted and sung as students moved from space to space. The chant "silence is violence" was a rhythmic call-and-response, a loud message to those who sat watching from their seats in the student center or memorial union. So many years after the civil rights era of the 1950s and 1960s, these millennials are communicating with the majority of people who look on curiously without participating. Another popular chant was taken from the pages of the Black Panther icon Assata Shakur's autobiography: "It is our duty to fight for our freedom/It is our duty to win/ We must love each other and support each other/We have nothing to lose but our chains" (2001, 52). This chant attested to the urgency that was powerfully exemplified in Butler's hunger strike. As the students marched past the disapproving glares of respectable black folks, offended white folks, and the Thomas Jefferson statue, their collective voices in these chants declared their intent to keep pushing through.

When the chants died down, silence would follow, and then one of the leaders would start a song, something meaningful and motivational. Traditional civil rights staples like "We Shall Overcome" were replaced with new songs such as Kendrick Lamar's "Alright" and the song's hook, "We gon' be alright," which became this generation's modern-day civil rights anthem. Released in July 2015, "Alright" arrived just in time to serve as the anthem for the nationwide movement. The accompanying video for the song was a reflection of the current political and social landscape of the United States. Much of the video is presented like a short documentary film as Lamar places himself above the city, watching from the precarious vantage point of a streetlight. This allows him (and the viewer) to watch the troubling pathological activities of police presence in urban spaces. At the end of the footage, a police officer watches him, aims, and shoots Lamar's character off his pedestal. As his body plummets in slow motion, we are urged to think about the reality that all the officer had to do was aim with his finger, a symbol of the systemic nature of these problems. In addition, we continue to hear and, therefore, consider the irony in the haunting chorus of "We gon' be alright." When Lamar's body lands, the camera zooms in on his face. He smiles at us, signifying a mixture of hope and cynicism in a future for which we must continue to fight. In other words, the artist is dead, but the music, representing the struggle, lives on.

Like "We Shall Overcome," Lamar's "Alright" has an internal focus on motivating those involved in the spiritual and physical dimensions of the movement. His lyrics rise to the occasion, updating the context to reflect contemporary issues with police brutality and the murder of young black people: "And we hate popo, when they kill us dead in the street for sure." As Lamar repeats the refrain, "We gon' be alright," he calls out to his "niggas." This is an interesting detail because when members of the community wrote to the local paper to comment on the story about Payton Head, a number of them expressed their confusion that if "they" use the N-word in their hip hop, why do "they" get offended when it is used by whites? This line of reasoning is problematic at best. When Lamar says "nigga" here, it is different from the word spat out against black folks on campus. The intention behind the word adds to the context for the meaning. Underscoring the nuanced use of the N-word, the ethnomusicologist Cheryl Keyes explains, "When used as a term of endearment among black speakers, 'nigga' is reclaimed, referring to one's buddy, neighborhood friend, and if spoken by a female MC, a male lover. However, the meaning of this term is solely determined by the adjective or possessive that precedes it" (2002, 137). Like so many members of the hip hop generation, Lamar's use of "nigga" signifies community and camaraderie while white racists' use of "nigger" is a throwback to slavery, hatred, and oppression.

As they marched, gathered, and congregated, the students would constantly break into the chorus of the song: "We gon' be alright!" Repeatedly they would sing, shout, chant this refrain. Although the students did not include the N-word in their chants, everybody who knew the song was aware that Lamar uses this word as a punctuation, as a term of endearment and solidarity, directed at those who embrace it as part of their sociocultural identity, which not everyone can claim. At the end of the spring semester, for their annual Black Love Week, the Legion of Black Collegians created a remake video linking the song to the unique Mizzou movement. As the only faculty member asked to participate, I was struck by the passion and commitment that each participant injected into the creative process. The students threw themselves into the process, which allowed them to rephrase and reinterpret Lamar's original piece while not quite changing the lyrics. The student videographers asked each participant to pick a verse or a phrase, look into the camera, and articulate the message for our community.[2]

Hip hop, and Kendrick Lamar's work in particular, represents a musical culture that relates to millennials; however, gospel music has had a wide and consistent appearance in black activist spaces and would also serve this generation's activism as well. In conjunction with the black church, gospel music has always been critical to any movements that black folks have led in the United States. The Mizzou case was interesting because gospel music was mostly not featured during the days of work in marches and protests. Leaders were mindful about the different faiths that were represented among the growing number of allies in the camp or in other spaces. I watched more white students joining the black students and other students of color. These new allies looked nervous but excited to hold hands and join the movement.

However, each night at the camp, the black student leaders would direct all to form a protective prayer circle around the camp, and they would take turns praying for love, for peace, for justice, and for their brother Jonathan, who was still in the midst of his hunger strike. Often, the prayer warriors went into the spirit, they would cry out, fall down, and wail through the prayer. One night I stepped in to prevent the well-meaning white counselors from rushing in to intervene. "That girl is having a nervous breakdown," a counselor exclaimed. I told her to just wait on the sidelines because this was "church." Some of the white students, new to this movement or to the reality of black life, grew even more nervous. As people held hands one dark, chilly night, there was a lull in the prayers and two African American women began to sing Hezekiah Walker's "I Need You to Survive." It was the right choice of song because it had spiritual and practical intent. As Mellonee Burnim explains, the double entendre that serves as a vital element in most spirituals and gospel songs sends more than one message about the lives and experiences of the singers (1985). Walker's popular song focuses on both a higher power as well as the very present physical power of allies for the movement. The lead singers at the camp on the quad filled the space with the beautiful melody of the song, and the rest of the circle of at least a hundred people sang along. The circle was strong as everyone held hands and allowed themselves to believe the words of Walker's song, expressing the sentiment that each person was needed and important, and that in the end each person was part of a larger whole. This song communicated clearly to the student activists that their struggle was supported, and to these new allies who finally understood that they were welcome.

INDIVIDUALS: PERSONAL ANTHEMS DURING THE STORM

In addition to the Black Lives Matter movement, our student movement at Mizzou and perhaps particularly the activism of our black student athletes, inspired the San Francisco 49ers' quarterback Colin Kaepernick to protest in the 2016 season, choosing to take a knee during the national anthem. His protest was a reminder that this national song has always been problematic for many African American athletes, as seen when John Carlos and Tommie Smith raised their gloved fists on the podium at the 1968 Mexico City Olympics. Kaepernick's action pointed to, among other things, the overlooked third verse of the anthem, which references slaves and reminds us that Francis Scott Key, writer of "The Star-Spangled Banner," was himself a slave master and an anti-abolitionist. In an advertisement for a slave he was selling, he posted "valuable slave for sale. William is a likely fellow, a good coachman and house servant" (Leepson 2014, 107).

Knowing this, Kaepernick's action urged, how does the descendent of a slave accept this song with pride without questioning the treatment of his community in the twenty-first century? The anthem is also referenced in a 1989 classic album, Janet Jackson's *Rhythm Nation 1814*. She deliberately included the year 1814 in the title, reminding consumers of the year "The Star-Spangled Banner" was written by Key. In so doing, Jackson provides a critique of the anthem's inherent inability to fully include those who were considered not quite as equal as others. In the title track she asserts "join voices in protest/ to social injustice/ . . . we are a part of the rhythm nation." In his 1952 book on national anthems, Paul Nettl concludes that "The Star-Spangled Banner" "is doubtless one of the great national anthems" (1952, 12). However, the question that Colin Kaepernick, Janet Jackson, and all our young Mizzou activists ask is for whom is this anthem truly great? Does the realization of American citizenship truly encompass all today?

Compare the responses of two R&B/soul singers when asked to comment on Kaepernick's protest. The African American soul singer Anthony Hamilton responded, "I'm gonna take a little time away from the anthem until it starts feeling like it's for me. We need a new song, one that really speaks for all of us, or [we need to] bring some new life to the one that we have" (*Billboard* 2016). In contrast, faced with the same question, the white American soul singer Jojo, who is comfortable appropriating black music, said, "When I sing the national anthem, I'm thinking of the veterans in my family, and I completely respect Colin's stance to bring awareness to black people who are still facing injustice, and I really do respect it. But for me, I'm just, I enjoy singing the song" (*Billboard* 2016). These varied positions on the national anthem are logical in a country where the embers of segregation and Jim Crow still glow, with the potential at every turn to spark up into a furnace. That activists like the Mizzou students turn away from national songs like these is no surprise. Yet songs and their messages of empowerment and pride remain a critical part of the movement, which is why I became interested in activists' personal song choices.

I noticed that when the Mizzou activists were resting or not in strategy meetings, that their headphones were always on their heads, and their earbuds were in their ears. This generation has grown up with headphones and the notion of individualized, personally curated music. Intrigued by what personal choices were bringing them through the storm of a tense period in their lives, I asked them what they were listening to. Without exception, they said they were deliberate in choosing the music that would get them through each next day. Payton Head, who had an adamant response to the perpetual racist environment of the university he loves, cited "There's Hope" by India.Arie as a personal, musical refuge. The song is a bright, uplifting tale of perspective and instruction to recalibrate one's sense of possibilities. In her usual straightforward style, India.Arie explains that folks should "take back their power." Her lesson to "stand up for your rights" fits the energy that emanated from Payton and the other students of the movement. His other choice comes from Janelle Monáe's *The Electric Lady* album and while different in terms of its soundscape, his chosen song from that work still reflects his gravitation toward strong messages and upbeat music. The title track of that Afro-futuristic, funk-infused album beams the listeners out from the difficult center of struggle. "Q.U.E.E.N.," the hit single from that album, shows Monáe and Erykah Badu redefining a space for marginalized folks. The title of the song, according to Monáe, is an acronym for

Queer, Untouchables, Emigrants, Excommunicated, and Negroid. It is a fitting anthem for a leader who put the campus above himself (Payton Head, interview with author, November 2015).

Danielle Walker, the woman who started the #RacismLivesHere movement, an important precursor for the part of the movement that gained national attention, told me she was listening to Nas's untiled 2013 album, in particular the song titled "N****r." For Danielle, a master's student, Nas's didactic words provide history and empowerment. "We were scholars long before there were colleges," Nas insists in this assertive statement that highlights the great history of African civilization and the resilience of African Americans (Danielle Walker, interview with author, November 2015).

Another graduate student, Maxwell Little, a core member of CS1950, revealed that he was listening to Stevie Wonder's "Love's in Need of Love Today" from the album *Songs in the Key of Life*. I was surprised by the choice of this song from the mid-1970s, but as I thought about this song, it became clear that Wonder's classic provides a soulful and timeless reflection on friendship and love, two critical elements needed for the continued work that these students were engaged in together. Even though this song was Maxwell's personal choice, it was a reminder, indeed an admonition, that the movement, to be successful, had to be infused with love, peace, and unity (Facebook Messenger correspondence with Maxwell Little, November 2015).

For a doctoral student named Reuben Faloughi, also a member of CS1950, "Charade" by D'Angelo and the Vanguard provided his inspirational, musical interlude. Instrumentally, this track returns to funky rhythms, reminiscent of Parliament Funkadelic and Prince, and sends its own revolutionary message and aligns with Reuben's identity as an activist, scholar, and musician (Reuben Faloughi, email correspondence with author, November 2015).

To many, Jonathan Butler was one of the central participants in the movement. His experience was both public and private because of his choice to embark on a hunger strike. He confirmed that music was a refuge: "My go-to music genre is definitely a tie between gospel and rap but the past two months I have been really inspired by Andy Mineo's album *Uncomfortable* and Nina Simone's album *Nina Simone's Finest Hour.*" It is satisfying to know that Simone's albums inspired this twenty-first-century activist because her explicitly political songs like "Mississippi Goddam" and "Four Women" set a spotlight on the plight of African Americans generally and of women in particular. Jonathan's choice of Mineo, an artist who mixes hip hop and Christianity, signifies the scope of his reach from old-school to a more contemporary music. The title track on *Uncomfortable* deftly critiques racism in this "postracial" America. He concludes, "Jesus wouldn't act like that" (Jonathan Butler, Facebook messenger correspondence with author, November 2015).

It came as no surprise that even in their quiet time, on their own, some of the activists cited Lamar's "Alright," a song that, as already described, the collective sang often. Undergraduate Marshall Allen explained, "This speaks to the determination and perseverance of us as Black people to keep moving forward because literally . . . ; we gon' be alright. This is like the black activist national anthem." Another member of CS1950, Asha Bashir also chose "Alright." She expanded on the reasons for this as the song that inspired her during the most difficult times that fall:

> I did not become familiar with this particular song until I became involved with Concerned Student 1950. In many situations, I am often referred to as the optimist. I look for the good in the bad and am always reinforcing to others to worry less and to have faith in God because after all, everything happens for a reason. "Alright" is a song that relates to this; it provides a sense of hope and reassurance for a promising future in the midst of the challenges, pain, and struggles that Black people face day in and day out. Despite disparities, it pushes listeners to realize that our fight towards progression in the direction of racial equality is not over and that in the end, we gon' be alright. "Alright," although not a physical place, became my safe haven. Whenever I was feeling down throughout this difficult time, I resorted to playing this song. It never failed to uplift my spirits and would constantly remind me that with solidarity and support for and from my people that we could and would never lose. (Asha Bashir, interview with author, November 2015)

It was clear to me that in the midst of a heavily saturated music market, where Drake, Rihanna, Big Sean, and Future are popular, the Mizzou activists mined for the music that would make the most sense to their experiences as black liberation fighters. These anthems serve as the soundtrack to the struggle. In *Anthems: Social Movements and the Sound of Solidarity in the African Diaspora,* Shana Redmon presents these black anthems as "counter-anthems" and that listening to them is a "political act in performance because it mobilizes communal engagements that speak to misrecognition, false histories, violence, and radical exclusion" (2013, 2). Ava Duvernay exemplifies this notion in her film *Selma* (2014), in the scene where Martin Luther King Jr. needs to re-center, to cast away the stress that comes with the work of black liberation. Specifically, he calls the gospel singer Mahalia Jackson, and she sings him his favorite song, "Precious Lord," to sooth him. That moment was replicated by all these Mizzou activists, selecting carefully from a vast range of black music across genre and time. It is this music that brought them through the tensest period in Mizzou's recent history, and it is this music that carried them out on the other side of the movement.

INDIVIDUALS: PERSONAL ANTHEMS AFTER THE STORM

A year after the movement, what became clear was the risk that our most active students took in working to bring change to our campus. In contention was their mental health, their peace of mind, their status as students in good standing, and, perhaps most importantly, their acceptance or ostracizing by family, friends, and foes. I stayed in touch with many of them and knew the toll that the movement had taken on them, so I asked them what music had brought them through the year. I was reminded that a focus on anthems is a productive way to think about this eternal struggle, this enduring movement, our troubling racial and racist history. A focus on these public and personal anthems can shed light on the activists and the personal journeys during and after the most intense moments of the movement.

Abigail Hollis was a member of CS1950. She graduated the semester after the movement and was accepted into the PhD program in psychology at Mizzou. She explained how music brought her through the year and helps her every day: "When I have things very together I get up in the mornings and listen to my morning playlist, which includes the happiest, most encouraging soul/R&B songs I could find. . . . The music calms me and I know the lyrics to most of the songs, so I can sing along, which is a self-soothing tactic for me." Her choices are, surprisingly, from earlier generations of black popular music: some of the most well-loved R&B standards, including Maze featuring Frankie Beverly, Whitney Houston, Michael Jackson, the Spinners, Lauryn Hill, and Stevie Wonder (Abigail Hollis, Facebook Messenger correspondence with author, October 16, 2016).

Storm Ervin, another member of CS1950, was just finishing an internship in Washington, DC, when I contacted her a year later to ask her about the music that had brought her through. She cited rapper Joey Bada$$'s "Devastated": "This is something I've listened to a lot lately. He discusses once being devastated and that he once thought he'd never make it. But now he's on his way to greatness. This song resonates with me because at one point I felt fighting against systems of oppression was becoming hopeless. Change really can't come from this protest and organizing. But now, after seeing things actually begin to change, I believe. And we're on our way to greatness: Greatness being liberation from all forms of oppression." (Storm Ervin, Facebook Messenger correspondence with author, October 17, 2016) These ideas are woven through the stark lines of Bada$$'s track: "Put my pain in a cadence/Turn my brain up a wavelength." The entire track is a statement of empowerment that makes sense for Storm.

Contradicting the tendency of media and academia to construct boundaries between genres, Storm connected Bada$$'s hip hop song to gospel music by also mentioning Yolanda Adams. Speaking of "Never Give Up" by Yolanda Adams, Storm said:

> Every lyric of that song is a message to me. It reassures me that my vision can change the world. When I'm feeling discouraged or devastated, this is my go to song to remember that in order to live and work toward a world without slavery in the form of prisons, capitalism, and racism, I can never give up. She talks about fulfilling divine purpose, which is something I'm beginning to see in myself. I have a purpose and I can't run from it. She talks about victories coming in time, which is an indicator that I need patience and to work through all odds. This song tells me to keep the dream of freedom alive, that I am capable, that I have everything I need to manifest the dream, and to never give up! (Storm Ervin, Facebook Messenger correspondence with author, October 17, 2016)

Returning to Reuben Faloughi a year later, who had cited D'Angelo during the movement, I was intrigued by his mention of Jay Electronica's "Better in Tune with the Infinite." The song is haunting and thought-provoking, beginning with samples from Elijah Muhammad, leader of the Nation of Islam. Then Electronica calmly lays down his rhymes, stringing a web of questions in settings from synagogues to churches, from Egypt to the bayous of New Orleans. Perhaps the most poignant line, "They might feel the music but could never ever feel me," is a reminder of the contradictory positionality of Jojo. Explaining his attraction to this song, Reuben states, "This has been my 'struggle' anthem since the protests. It validates the physical and psychological damage from the protests to now. It's an empowering reminder to keep moving forward in tune with the infinite. It's a very intentional track. Elijah Muhammad, Professor Marvel, no drums, Rhetoric, everything about this song is simple and raw. Like life. It's a struggle but as Electronica says, 'staring out the windows is for love songs and houseflies.'"

Of "Blackberry Molasses" by the 1990s R&B group Mista, Reuben explains, "This song highlights the raw experience of being Black in the U.S. There are few songs in my mind that express this type of vulnerability and put black racial trauma into perspective. As a counselor in training and a pretty resilient Black male, sometimes it's easy to think mental health is abstract or its effects are minimal; however it's not true. Many of those involved with the protests, including myself, continue to struggle with the events from last semester and on-going stress, negativity from Mizzou community members, and triggers" (Reuben Faloughi, email correspondence with author, October 16, 2016).

When I asked Marshall Allen, a senior majoring in political science and black studies, what he was listening to, he thought for a while and then said he had been listening a lot to Chance the Rapper's new album *The Coloring Book*, which has become an album that is widely popular among African American millennials and others. Chance's mixture of gospel and hip hop seems to be compelling to a generation of Americans searching for innovative ways of expressing the frustrations of their reality. Now a PhD student at the University of Denver, Danielle Walker mentioned another popular contemporary album. She found solace in Beyoncé's *Lemonade*. "It is on constant repeat. Black womyn magic is what I'm seeking. . . . The unapologetic blackness I have been listening to has been very affirming of myself; and loving myself. Listening to music that affirms my identity is like putting on a super cloak to be able to navigate this white supremacist world. It helps me to thrive" (Danielle Walker, interview with author, November 2015). Both *Coloring Book* and *Lemonade* were released in 2016 to critical acclaim and wide approval from a range of fans. Like Kendrick Lamar's "Alright," Walker's song choices represent a trend reviving in popular music as these songs adeptly and unequivocally take on the most urgent issues that face this generation of black folks.

MUSIC IN THE ACADEMY

While activists were utilizing music on a collective and individual level, it is also important to discuss how the institution, the University of Missouri, was affected in a unique way by the music of the movement. In the spring of 2016, the only black graduate student in the music conducting program of the School of Music, Ernest (EJ) Harrison, was moved to compose a new piece for the University Singers. EJ had been watching from his position on the sidelines, mentally affected if not physically involved in the marches and protests. He was inspired to write a new piece of music for the predominantly white university choir, one that reflected the movement and the struggle of black students on their particular campus. The choral conductor, my colleague Dr. Paul Crabb, was faced with a choice of whether or not to include the new piece in the spring concert. He could have said that the program for the spring concert was set. It would have been easy and perhaps wise to do so, as donors are a delicate crowd who do not appear to want to be bothered with issues of race. Instead Paul encouraged EJ in his composing and invited him to conduct this particular song.

Paul privileged EJ's piece, "Anthem," by putting it at the end of the program. The fact that EJ titled his piece thus was telling of the commentary that he, too, like Janet Jackson and Colin Kaepernick, was reflecting on the validity of the national anthem for all Americans. During the concert, EJ's "Anthem" was a showstopper. It is a beautifully artful fusion of the State of Missouri anthem with the old civil rights song "We Shall Overcome." It begins with some of the jarring quotes from our local paper and local community, a showcase of racist and xenophobic reactions to black students. These quotes are shouted out into the silence by choir members who are sitting among the audience. Then there is the sound of commotion and noise, effective symbolism for the chaotic environment surrounding any social movement. When the commotion dies down, the choir takes over in a beautifully balanced mixture of the voice sections and of the two songs. Its eerie notes remind the listeners of the history of the state, its problematic position in the slavery debate, and the important trajectory between the historical and contemporary moments. This alliance between EJ and Professor Paul Crabb gives us a model and a symbolic gesture that might attempt to bridge the racial gap. By working together, Paul and EJ produced a new anthem that urged our music students and the entire community to challenge the status quo and to think critically about the rights and responsibilities of true and equal citizenship.

Another way in which music has featured on an institutional level appears in the mandatory diversity program, Citizenship@Mizzou, which all incoming freshmen and graduate students have to attend. When I was asked to design the program, I decided to include music in the session, which also includes brief lectures by faculty. By taking other classic anthems and sharing them at the Citizenship@Mizzou sessions, we are asking students to engage with race and identity through music and culture. For example, they listen to Bob Dylan's "Blowin' in the Wind," Marvin Gaye's "What's Going On," John Lennon's "Imagine," and the Black Eyed Peas' "Where Is the Love?" Talking Drum is a band of Mizzou student musicians, who came together to assist me in this venture. They represent the impulse of this generation to weave music into the movement and to utilize musical culture to impact and change the most problematic aspects of American culture.

Conclusion: Black Music as a Tool to Combat Racism

There was a huge backlash and multiple programs had to be mounted to help our community deal with the turmoil. One night, I moderated a discussion after the screening of *Freedom Summer*, a film that highlights the coalition that was built when white students went down to Mississippi in 1963 to help black activists in their fight for voting rights. That evening, I asked people to think about how that moment connects to us at Mizzou. Two of the most poignant responses were from white audience members who told us they were raised in prejudiced homes. When I urged them to think about what made them progressive, they both reflected for a moment, and then an older white man said he heard Aretha Franklin, and she led him to the blues. That helped him to branch away from a family rooted in generations of racism. The other person happens to be a professor at Mizzou. I followed up with her afterward:

I was raised with liberal Democratic values but as a teenager I became, for lack of a better word, radicalized and I do think that music played a part in that transformation. . . . I hated the white-privileged, middle-class suburban world I grew up in—I was a big Janis Joplin fan & she opened up new worlds for me; she spoke in interviews about the artists who had influenced her—Bessie Smith, Billie Holiday—and I learned everything I could about them. I used to check out records and tapes from the library—mostly blues & jazz. I have a memory of getting into Mahalia Jackson's music and my (Jewish) family thinking I was a little crazy. (Mizzou faculty member, Facebook Messenger correspondence with author, November 30, 2015) [3]

And then her story took a twist, which highlighted the intersectionality that must accompany any serious thinking about social justice activism.

I would be remiss if I didn't talk about sexuality and its importance in my story. I mentioned that my family was "liberal." My mother was an artist and a free thinker in many ways but also someone who was a product of her time and place and therefore conservative around certain issues. To compress a very complicated and traumatic part of my history, I was disowned by my family when I came out as gay at 19 in my sophomore year of college. It was brutal to no longer be welcome in my own home and to have my mother write me that she wished I were dead. Heartbroken and confused, I conformed to my family's expectations and went in the closet for many years. I came out again when I was in graduate school and was disowned all over again. The bravery, beauty, and intelligence of sexually nonconforming women artists like Bessie Smith and Billie Holiday have inspired me and given me strength over the years. (Mizzou faculty member, Facebook Messenger correspondence with author, November 30, 2015)

These experiences connect with what LeRoi Jones/Amiri Baraka said: "Black music is the result of the attitude, and the stance. . . . Negroes made blues and others did not, because of the Negroes' peculiar way of looking at the world" (2010, 25). And that ultimately gives nonblack listeners a window into a world beyond their borders.

As campuses like Mizzou, Yale, and Princeton, and as cities like Chicago, Baltimore, and Ferguson, attempt to bounce back from these crises that sprouted from the hundreds of years of systemic racism, they are facing an uphill task. Historian Robin D. G. Kelley reflects on the depth of time within which this problem has endured, "None of this brutality is new. In my fifty-three years on this earth, I've experienced not a wave but a continuous stream of police violence that has never let up" (2016, 18). The challenge for cities and campuses all across the United States is to figure out why existing approaches to programming to raise awareness to racism and other forms of discrimination have not changed minds and hearts.

As I have watched the Mizzou movement unfold and as I have been involved in the aftermath, I have heard a number of comments from people outside the movement, those who have never had to think about race because they have either ignored or refused to acknowledge the reality of the full spectrum of American life and culture. Often, these folks exclaim that they never knew any of this was going on, and that, in fact, "All Lives Matter." Lately, my reaction has been to point them in the direction of black music. The rich layers of this unique cultural expression offer a priceless lens through which black life is illuminated so that #BlackLivesMatter may become valid to those who live inside and outside the community.

NOTES

1. According to the university archives, the denials of admission to African Americans came around the 1930s. The first African American student in 1950 was Gus T. Ridge. "Significant Dates in the History of the University of Missouri," http://muarchives.missouri.edu/sigdates.html

2. The Legion of Black Collegians video can be viewed at https://m.youtube.com/watch?v=VsI1It-ZcAQ

3. The faculty member asked that she not be identified by name.

WORKS CITED

Billboard. 2016. "Alicia Keys, Anthony Hamilton and More Singers Rethink National Anthem amid Kaepernick Protest." October 14, 2016.

Burnim, Mellonee. 1985. "The Black Gospel Music Tradition: A Complex of Ideology, Aesthetic, and Behavior." In More than Dancing: Essays on Afro-American Music and Musicians, edited by Irene Jackson Brown, 147–167. Westport, CT: Greenwood.

Guralnick, Peter. 1986. Sweet Soul Music: Rhythm and Blues and the Southern Dream of Freedom. New York: Back Bay Books.

Heavin, Jenese. 2010. "Two Arrested in Cotton Ball Incident." Columbia Daily Tribune, March 3, 2010. http://www.columbiatribune.com/news/crime/two-arrested-in-cotton-ball-incident/article_d9781cd7-52ee-5f18-801b-a66de6d6720c.html.

Jones, LeRoi. 2010. Black Music. New York: Akashic.

Kelley, Robin D. G. 2016. "Thug Nation: On State Violence and Disposability." In Policing the Planet: Why the Police Crisis Led to Black Lives Matter, edited by Jordan Camp and Christina Heatherton, 15–33. New York: Verso.

Keyes, Cheryl. 2002. *Rap Music and Street Consciousness*. Champagne: University of Illinois Press.

Leepson, Marc. 2014. *Francis Scott Key: A Life*. New York: Palgrave Macmillan.

Lowery, Wesley. 2016. *"They Can't Kill Us All": The Story of Black Lives Matter*. New York: Penguin.

Maultsby, Portia K. 1989. "Soul Music: Its Sociological and Political Significance." In *American Popular Music Volume 2: The Age of Rock*, edited by Timothy Schreurer, 168–178. Bowling Green, OH : Bowling Green State University Popular Press.

Nettl, Paul. 1952. *National Anthems*. New York: Storm Publishers.

Redmon, Shana. 2013. *Anthems: Social Movements and the Sound of Solidarity in the African Diaspora*. New York: New York University Press.

Shakur, Assata. 2001. *Assata: An Autobiography*. Chicago: Lawrence Hill.

Stevenson, Bryan. 2014. *Just Mercy: A Story of Justice and Redemption*. New York: Spiegel & Grau.

Taylor, Keeanga-Yamahtta. 2016. *From #BlackLivesMatter to Black Liberation*. Chicago: Haymarket.

STEPHANIE SHONEKAN is Associate Professor of Ethnomusicology and Black Studies at the University of Missouri. She is author of *Soul, Country and the USA: Race and Identity in American Music* and *The Life of Camilla Williams, African American Classical Singer and Opera Diva*.

TWO

BLACK MATTERS: BLACK FOLK STUDIES AND BLACK CAMPUS LIFE

Fernando Orejuela

AMERICAN COLLEGE STUDENTS AND FACULTY members are challenging the institutional racism of American higher education and their respective institutes' muddled approaches to practicing inclusivity and promoting the value of diversity. This chapter addresses the passively hostile, teaching environment of a big state university campus and the practice of teaching about racial inequality through hip hop musical communities in an attempt to bring to light the experiences of teaching in the midst of racial unrest in the United States. I propose to expand on common problems that are faced by many of us who teach critical thinking courses on diversity issues, and I follow with a reflection of the pedagogical plan I had set forth for my own course. A couple of the many leading questions I had to ask myself when a group of us first gathered for a roundtable on music and the Black Lives Matter (BLM) movement at the Society of Ethnomusicology annual conference that I still confront include the following:

- What role do we have as scholars to refuse to accept the assertion of a European collegiate universe, which placates the dominant Eurocentric student body?
- What do pedagogies centered on art, resistance, racial violence, microaggressions, and its aftermath look like? More importantly, how do we assess the results?

This chapter is broken in two parts: inspirational events and actionable attempts. The former brings to the readers' attention some reflections of experiences at the university level in our attempts to "do" diversity on campus and embrace a color-blind racialization of our student body. The latter is my work in progress, engaging both with critical race theory and theories of communication and performance, as applied to ways that hip hop artists engage with the discourses of the Black Lives Matter movement, and with students' understanding of those engagements, followed by an analysis of the outcomes. My effort is a move toward putting activist teaching to use.

Part 1: A Reflection

Before I start, I believe some context is necessary to situate us better with my first question. I am a Senior Lecturer in Ethnomusicology and Folklore as well as an Adjunct Professor in African American and African Diaspora Studies. Currently, I cycle three courses on hip hop studies in addition to my other required courses. My mentor in ethnomusicology, Portia K. Maultsby, started teaching a rap music course at Indiana University (IU) in 1989, becoming the first scholar in the nation to do so. In the fall of 1998, I became her teaching assistant for the 400-level rap music course—an issue-based course that I took over and continue to teach. The demographic makeup of that particular class is pertinent to the issues I will raise here. In the fall semester, eighty undergraduate students and six graduate students were enrolled in the course. What I found most interesting was that almost half the student body was African American and one Nigerian (my colleague, Stephanie Shonekan). This impressed me because in the late 1990s only about 7 percent of the Indiana University undergraduate students identified as black and my previous teaching assistantship, the Introduction to Folklore course, had left an impact on me. In that class, we had three hundred students enrolled every semester for the four semesters that I taught, and only one of the approximate twelve hundred students was African American. Clearly, the subject of rap music examined through a sociocultural historical lens in an academic setting was especially attractive to African American students.

In the following spring semester, we had eighty undergraduates enrolled in the rap music class, but our demographics changed considerably. We had five African American women and one Latina, and the rest of the student body was Euro-American. Statistics since the 1990s, such as the following data reported by Chuck Phillips in his *Los Angeles Times* article from 1992, marked the shift in the consumption of rap music to about 74 percent white, but the real impact that school year was the emergence of Eminem, who remains the most prodigious white rapper to date. I became the professor of record in 2003, and in 2005 I created a 200-level survey course that currently seats more than 250 students every semester and my 2014 book, *Rap and Hip Hop Culture,* is based on that course. By 2016, the demographics had not really changed at all for African Americans (7.5 percent) though the Latino population has more than tripled (7.2 percent), according to University Institutional Research and Reporting (2016). However, the classroom looks about the same as it did since that memorable paradigm shift in the spring of 1999. This history is important context for my approach in the classroom.

Another rather recent event that affected my thinking about teaching hip hop courses occurred in the fall of 2015. I was invited to participate on a panel for the popular music section at the American Musicological Society in Louisville, Kentucky. The roundtable was called "Culture Vultures and Teaching Hip Hop Courses." The title unnerved me, but since a former student had invited me to participate, I promised to do it. One of the recurring concerns made by the musicologists on the panel was the pressure by their home departments to teach a hip hop course. Ethnomusicologists typically study and teach about hip hop culture with the recognition that the musical component is a bona fide genre of the American experience and that it is culture that includes other artful expression and ideologies rooted in African America and the African diaspora. Within the field, we do not treat teaching hip hop studies as a side subject, a necessary evil that supports other courses like music theory or other traditional music courses that are struggling with enrollment. As I listened to the other participants of the roundtable I noticed that the concern was how not to be a culture vulture, yet the discussion of culture vulturism made no mention of hip hop music as an expression of black culture. Rather, it focused on interactive approaches to rap music, such as teaching dance moves or writing an original rap. While I support interactive approaches to teaching, and incorporate them into my curriculum, I argue that what I do, what I must do when I teach hip hop culture courses is culture work and not just "subculture" work. In other words, students are introduced to an ethnomusicological methodology to assess the emergence of hip hop as part of African American and African diasporic expressive cultures. Those of us who do culture work, especially in public spaces such as museums, festivals, concert series, and so forth, recognize that it is less about cultural appropriation and vulturism, and more about opportunities to address genre, aesthetics, culture, and history from a worldview that is not privileging or does not privilege the European model as the norm and all other systems of meaning as ethnic others and, therefore, as inferior or second tier.

For my small, upper-level hip hop course that seats about thirty students, I employ discussions of critical race theory, music-making, and social issues addressed in the work of hip hop artists (commercial, underground, and virtual). We also get down and do basic B-boy dance moves to learn through the body how style is acquired and that true competence is not easily mastered. We collect hip hop style graffiti around the Bloomington area, distinguishing it from tags, punk styles, rollers, scratchies, and stencils, and we engage in discussions regarding moral panics, free-walls versus outlaw art, and an ongoing commitment to a highly stylized, subversive tradition. I have a turntablist from Indianapolis, Ben "DJ Action Jackson" Jackson, demonstrate his craft and address the shifts into Serrato Scratch Live and laptop DJing as well as the shifting soundscapes that remain covered by the umbrella of hip hop musics. Finally, my students participate in an MC battle to learn, once again, through the body what it means to ride a beat, rep your crew, and perform a story in verse. The goal is not to create rap artists: most of my students struggle with the minimum competencies to manage the poetics and verbal dexterity that even the simplest pop-rap star—whom they comfortably critique so harshly—can do with ease. It puts talking over a beat into perspective and that not just anyone can do it. Engaging in creative praxis, learning through the body, is significant if you have a small class. It is not practical for my large class of 270 students. I must add that when I do engage in creative praxis I remind my students that we study performance, but we engage in "informance" and "edutainment": that is, an activity that is educational and entertaining, perhaps artistic, but not the fully realized artifacts of culture we study. In fact, unlike other performance classes in ethnomusicology, ours is not an ensemble. There is no public recital at the end of the semester: just the battle for classroom supremacy and bragging rights. Incorporating established "old school" folk forms is ideal and manageable for the small classroom environment, but those are not the most essential components of teaching hip hop studies. Hip hop elements—DJing, MCing, graffiti writing, and breaking—have moved translocally since the 1970s and not necessarily together. Furthermore, the issues that need to be discussed can be obscured when the focus becomes locked on style (song as text) and not culture.

The culture work I mentioned earlier is critical to my teaching. I have a commitment to meet the mission of Black Studies and the foundational work of my ethnomusicology and folklore study mentors. Make no mistake, when we say hip hop we have to make clear that we are talking about a black diasporic musical culture and not just subculture. Engaging in hip hop studies is *doing* activism. It creates a counterspace to express the narratives and soundscapes of the black experience by viewing people of the African diaspora as the subject of study and not the object. We have to talk about race critically, in American contexts for sure, and global contexts as well since hip hop has been mass-produced in all corners of the world.

I must ask my students to confront race through hip hop studies because it is easy for them to look at rap as just a style of music-making disconnected from human agency. Instead, the approach recognizes the intersectional systems potentiated within hip hop studies and discourses on race, especially because race operates on many levels, often simultaneously. Therefore, we have to discuss race and gender, race and sexuality, race and violence, race and social and economic mobility, race and the generation gap, race and ethnicity, race and . . . . We have to be sure to voice our pedagogical concerns with the subcultural condition and also allow space for other voices and realities within the struggles that are happening now in the proactive Black Lives Matter age, as evidenced in the narratives of Kendrick Lamar, the street violence tales in Chicago's drill rap scene, the sexual violence discussed in the lyrics of Angel Haze, and the ethnic awareness and consciousness-raising actions of Noname or Yasiin Bey changing their MC names. This pursuit lies at the base of the pedagogical mission of all those who teach hip hop in our contemporary academy.

I teach courses on race or ethnic studies in a predominantly white university. I imagine that many instructors teaching courses on race or ethnicity have encountered students suggesting or claiming that racism is over in the post-Obama age. At Indiana University, the following events were some ways that racism had "ended" in the academic year 2015–2016.

On an anonymous, safe-space application called Yik Yak, striking comments were posted after IU students who stood in solidarity with the protesting Mizzou students uploaded their picture in front of the Black Culture Center. For example, one anonymous student posted, "There's no racism at IU. Go back to Africa you Blafricanist." In that same week, the lives of our black students were threatened by an anonymous assailant who wrote, "If you're not white don't come to class today" (Lanich 2015). The threats appeared in our campus newspapers yet many of my students in the three courses I was teaching were largely unaware; furthermore, no alert was issued to my phone or email on the campus emergency alert system. In response to these events, the Black Graduate Student Organization held an emergency meeting at the end of the week. I attended with the chair of African American and African Diaspora Studies, and we remained silent in the audience because it was a student-run event and we were there for moral support. They invited the provost and the dean of students and requested the IU police to be present, given the threat to their lives. The Black Graduate Student Association president explained that the police declined the request because there was a basketball game at the same time as the meeting. The color-blind attitude of university administrators, colleagues, and students often render students of color and their concerns invisible.

While I understand my university's attempt at structuring diversity as a project, some of that attention to diversity is often most evident in the form of photos displayed prominently on brochures or campus-life posters. For example, one of my former graduate students appears on several posters and calendars promoting the sports recreation facilities. Additionally, one of our highest achieving black female students, a Wells Scholar, appears, front and center, on four different brochures for the Kelly School of Business. It would appear that the student body at IU is not so white despite the fact that the black student population has dropped every year since a peak of 8.3 percent in 2012. University impression management, I argue, is a problem. Compositional diversity is emphasized over inclusion. Tokenism is a problem, but it is treated like a solution. So how do I *un*-teach that?

PART 2: A PEDAGOGY OF UNTEACHING

Early in my career, even as a graduate student instructor, I had maintained that whenever I teach, communicating the importance of tolerance was one of the primary goals. I am committed to teaching the neglected life stories of underrepresented peoples in an academe that continues to favor individual achievements and histories of great political leaders and great wars or conquests. However, teaching tolerance was and is not enough. Acceptance is ideal, but comprehending this abstract thing we call equality, only obscurely imagined, is harder to achieve.

In response to the ongoing activities of the Black Lives Matter movement, the state in which my students' lives are impacted by the racial unrest on campus today, black musicians' response to the recurrence of violence to black bodies, and a commitment to challenge my students in my Diversity in U.S. courses, I attempt to incorporate basic tenets of critical race theory in my classroom. I focus on two tenets in particular: that "racism is ordinary, not aberrational" (Delgado and Stefancic 2012, 7) and the social construction thesis, which holds "that race and races are products of social thought and relations and not based on biological or genetic reality" (2012, 8). To undo the misleading messages that all is equal on the campus and American society at large, I devised a short writing assignment with two objectives for my students. The first was to navigate through the sometimes messy, in-betweenness of black music as commodity and black music as lived experience; the second was to demonstrate the ability to develop arguments, ideas, and opinions, grounded in rational analysis, about forms of hip hop musical expressions.

The objective is for students to begin to accept that they have already begun the process of decolonizing their listening habits by claiming rap music as their generation's music regardless of race, ethnicity, age, or gender; and to urge students to critique hegemonic racism (as well as other isms and phobias) in order to think critically about the modern world in which we live. It also asks them to unpack and compare the counternarratives introduced in class, such as tenets of black nationalism expressed in the works of early hip hop, like Grandmaster Flash and the Furious Five's "The Message" (1982) and Queen Latifah's "U.N.I.T.Y" (1992) or elements of the Black Panther Party for Self-Defense's ten-point plan in Public Enemy's "Bring the Noise" (1987) and Ice Cube's "Who Got the Camera?" (1992). Then we connect the past to a contemporary movement in the ongoing fight for human rights and the music they are streaming today, such as Kendrick Lamar's BLM anthem, "Alright" (2015), Noname's "Samaritan" (2013), and The Game's "Don't Shoot (Mike Brown Tribute)" (2014). In addition to applying materials from lecture and the textbook, I asked students to read Alicia Garza's "A Herstory of the #BlackLivesMatter Movement" (2014) to contextualize this current movement for civil rights with the ways in which rap artists negotiate and express social and political commitments to black resistance.

In the prompt, I offer the following headings that deal with the precepts outlined in Garza's explanation of the Black Lives Movement: Rap as Protest Music, Ghetto Strife and Conflict Today, Women as Object/Women as Subject in Hip Hop Today, and Challenging Notions about Gender. Each topic is matched with at least a pair of rap songs with options for students to venture out and choose different rap songs of their choice. In the 2015–2016 academic year, I tested the second short writing assignment of the semester. In reacting to these writing prompts, these students have an opportunity to apply and discuss ways of thinking about and communicating the concerns of the relational and interrelational complexities of cultural forms and ideologies as related to hip hop. Most students followed the guidelines, which pleased me, but there were students in the spring 2017 semester whose work attempted to blur the boundaries of the argument paper as genre and to manipulate the conventions of academic writing typically taught in first-year English composition in order to support better an alternative perspective that has yet to make its appearance in hip hop music-making. Such practices are becoming less unusual. In *Student Writing and Genre: Reconfiguring Academic Knowledge*, Fiona English refers to this phenomenon as regenring, and she argues that "a shift in genre allowed a shift in agency because the new genres allowed students to adopt or create new discursive identities" (2011, 131).[1] Below, I present at least two examples in which some kinds of shifting from one mode to another mode of writing occur.

In the fall of 2015, I tested the assignment in the same semester as the student-led activism at Mizzou, the Mike Brown case, and the other events mentioned earlier. Students addressed the query in the prompt, balancing the article by Garza with examples drawn mostly from the examples I provided, though some did take the option to use other rap songs to address one of the issues. The results, on average, were successful. Most students were able to connect song lyrics (and in some cases video footage) and current-day activism and protestations to the options provided or to other musical examples of their choosing. The analyses mostly stayed on target and contained, though there were a few interjections that "all lives matter" but those interjections were not fully developed. While there is nothing wrong with positing that all lives matter—in fact, all lives should and do matter—that is not the context for the rap artists addressing street violence, sexual assault, police brutality, and homophobia in their narratives. The context is specifically intersected with a black identity and placed or spaced in the United States. In class, I encouraged students who wished to present an argument to support #AllLivesMatter in contemporary, hip hop songs but they had to provide rap lyrics or rap videos that supported their argument. At the time of this publication, there are no rap songs that I can name; however, an antiblack, extremist rap song, ultimately against both Black Lives Matter and All Lives Matter, emerged in 2017. The song appeared in a viral video attributed to a student at Old Dominion University and referred to as "White Girl, White Power," but, again, her rap does not support the #AllLivesMatter argument because the rapper advocates lynching and killing black people, and she freely uses a racial slur to discredit Black History Month. In the video she sometimes wears a President Trump mask and a T-shirt that says "My president is white," totes a gun, and puts out her cigarette on a cocktail napkin that reads "BLACK LIVES MATTER."[2] Certainly, the students from 2015–2016 would not have had this song as a frame of reference.

In the following spring semester of 2016, I repeated the assignment. In the second attempt, a few students responded in ways that went beyond the more common "all lives matter" interjections we read in the previous semester to ones that expressed opinions aggressively doubting racism today as in this example:

> I think the entire #BlackLivesMatter is such an unfair movement and the fact that people genuinely got upset when the #AllLivesMatter is complete bullshit and entirely parallels the same thought that white people are suppressing black people. Is there still racism existing in the world today, probably, but there is also murder and rape and plenty of other awful events that occur that go unnoticed. I was raised in a society where race was never an issue and was not even a second thought, and I feel pretty strongly that the majority of the

millennial generation does not have an overall sense of racism either. How can people get upset saying that all lives equally matter rather than isolating black lives and putting them on a different pedestal, all that does is increase the rift and add to the issue. (Student One [name withheld], 2016)

Another example from a student suggested that some black victims deserve to be shot, supporting his opinion with a hypothetical situation. "If I was a white cop and a white youth pulls a 'finger-gun' from his jacket in a confrontational situation, I likely have shot him too—actions have consequences" (Student Two). While still a minority in our class of 270 students, such positions were more prevalent in the spring semester and were stated far more vehemently than typically allotted in any academic paper, regardless of discipline. Aside from the typical writing problems in both examples (grammar issues, not checking spelling and punctuation), something else is happening.

Disagreement, of course, is encouraged in the argument paper, yet these types of discourses or hypothetically evidenced statements not substantiated by facts resembled much newer computer-mediated communication: flaming in the former, social media sharing in the latter. Flaming is a mean-spirited, insulting activity shared between persons over the internet for the general, virtual community to read; flaming expressions often involve the use of profanity and can range in style from a quick quip to a lengthy diatribe. Short-lived, social media postings, shared liberally and trending in a given, immediate moment on students' Twitter feeds and other social media portals, create a space that understands a democratic subjectivity as universally applicable without self-reflection or qualifying one's possible myopic perspective. As a writing convention on the internet, flaming and unchecked postings on social media are permissible and endured. So why not employ the practice in academic writing? Term "papers" have become largely paperless activities and often composed online in a text-entry box. The argument paper as genre becomes blurred, regardless of the writing conventions one learns in a first-year English writing class.

The attitudinal change from one semester to the next was troublesome even though it was the perspective of a small minority. The prompt had not changed, once again it asked students to identify the #BlackLivesMatter debates in relations to various themes in rap music today. The same teaching assistants from the fall semester brought to my attention the major change in tone and attitude toward the assignment. In fact, in the earlier draft of my paper, I had only focused on the second semester's negative responses. My assessment attempts to match those *other* voices ghosting around students' essays. In the classic sociolinguistic text *Explorations in the Ethnography of Speaking*, Keith Basso strayed from vocalizing utterances to examine how writing and language studies are not so different. In his essay, Basso proposed for scholars to focus on writing as a form of communicative activity with primary emphasis on "an understanding of social and cultural factors that influence the ways written codes are actually used" ([1974] 1989, 426). Basso's approach to an ethnography of writing aided my first attempt to begin addressing these student essays, but he could not have anticipated the communicative technologies we engage in today. More recent works looking at student writing from a contemporary sociolinguistic perspective of genre, interdiscursivity, and entextualization in higher educational settings (English 2011; Wortham and Reyes 2014) as well as the roles of social media and interdiscursivity (Bauman 2004; Jackson 2013; Lomborg 2013) have been especially helpful references to address the blurred or regenred, and so have works on constructing narratives and gossiping (Fludernik [1996] 2010; Miller 2005).

The argument paper as blurred genre has been reshaped into the telling of "my opinion." The writing is not fully autonomous, but co-constructed with other audible, ghosting voices to explain a phenomenon without constraining one's words to the structural systems of formal, academic writing conventions. The argument paper I assigned advocates intertextuality, beginning with the fact that the writer's text is supported by other texts. Richard Bauman explains: "Whether by the attribution of literary influence, of the identification of literary sources and analogues, or the ascription of traditionality, or the allegation of plagiarism or copy right violation—or, indeed, by any of a host of other ways of literary texts depends in significant part on the alignment of texts to prior texts and the anticipation of future texts has drawn critical—and ideological—attention to this reflexive dimension of discursive practice (2004, 1)." This short writing assignment provides a particular insight into intertextuality, and how popular music text, digital literacies, and understanding are produced at many levels. My use of ghosting voices is meant to be playful. Rules of academic writing insist that the writer document every viewpoint referenced to support a position and use standardized citation conventions. Academic writing is a heteroglossic, text-based enterprise, attempting to orient readers to reconcile the writer's now-said to the already-said. Through citations, such ghosts are made visible. My concern is when the already-said text is not documented and, therefore, the ghosts are present but are not made visible. Applying the way that Fiona English problematizes the way instructors create a prompt (2011, 133), I do instruct students to look both outward to a musical cultural context, rap music, and inward toward a disciplinary one, such as the assessment of correspondence to Garza's political position to create the platform for BlackLivesMatter.

In the fall semester of 2015, the Mizzou student protests were still in the news. Furthermore, Sandra Bland, Freddie Gray, Tamir Rice, and Mike Brown among others were still newsworthy, and perhaps that helped foster empathetic voices in those students' essays. By the spring semester of 2016 we witnessed a rise in aggressive arguments for a perceived, neglected disenfranchised group, the white middle class, which coincided with emerging alt-right perspectives becoming fashionable on youth-oriented, social media spaces and college campuses, and due to political campaigning strategies that encouraged repeating unproven facts with no consequences.[3] Those trending, mediated events were more readily available than old-fashioned media sources.

Narrativization attempts to negotiate the perceived texts that ghost around a communicative event—such as an argument paper—in such a way that micro- and sometimes macroaggressive racist sentiments are self-confirming ways to tolerate racial injustice in the United States today. Monika Fludernik ([1996] 2010) views narrativization as a process in which narrativity is attached to the idea of experientiality—the tapping into a recipient's familiarity with a given experienced event through cognitive parameters. It is that experientiality that helps assert spontaneous narratives of experience, such as gossip and rumor on social media spaces, and it can be understood here as the prototype for all subsequent development of mediums and forms of narrative. Similarly, Richard Bauman in *A World of Others' Words* addresses Mikhail Bakhtin's proposition that "each act of textual product presupposes antecedent texts and anticipates prospective ones" (2004, 4). "For Bakhtin," Bauman explains, "dialogue, the orientation of the now-said to the already-said and the to-be-said is ubiquitous and foundational, comprehending all of the ways that utterances can resonate with other utterances and constitutive of consciousness, society, and culture" (5).

For the purpose of defining the written text to construct a method for students to discuss and address race and diversity as concepts linked to the everyday social lives in which we live and not simply studying text (in the form of song lyrics) that exist superorganically, I adapt Bauman's conception of genre as "one order of [communicative] style, a constellation of systematically related, co-occurant formal features and structures that serves as a conventionalized orienting framework for the production and reception of discourse" (2004, 3).[4] In an era of reposting others' words as if they were our words on social media—that is, the logic of reposting an expression suggests this other person's words are words I would have stated myself—we create texted or typed expressions that behave like orally relayed utterances. While normalized in oral communication, utterances are subject to entextualizing another's words, and we accept a stated text to circulate and circulate, over and over. As Bauman observes, "The iterability for texts, then, constitutes one of the most powerful bases for the potentiation and production of intertextuality" (4).

In my examples, the "utterances" are not vocalized; rather they are cyber utterances and their "already-said" context allows for students to continue practicing microaggressions and pardon detrimental acts against certain members of the US population as a result of color-blindness ideologies. Student One "was raised in a society where race was never an issue and was not even a second thought, and . . . feel[s] pretty strongly that the majority of the millennial generation does not have an overall sense of racism either." Those previously stated social media feeds perform like rumors and gossip in oral circulation where facts do not have to be checked and are typically circulated among a smaller group of similar-minded, online circle of friends. In the case of Student One, he supports his statement as a member of a monolithic, millennial generation that is not perceived as diverse. Note that these written texts are not as subject to plagiarism so much as to what Noel Jackson calls "acts of transgressive and nontransgressive intertextuality" (2013). Much like communications on social media, words can be lifted verbatim and recirculated without attribution. Paraphrasing is even more permissible.

Furthermore, these public communications by way of social media are infused with private hypotheses for coping with uncertainties and anxieties. That is, passing rumors perceived as credible (including outrageous stories) is an attempt by the rumormonger to help listeners—very generously and without asking an audience if they need help coping—by providing a rationale for behavior that produces the anxiety (Rosnow 2001). Sociologist Dan E. Miller adds that, more than rumor, gossip is in play and tends to have an "inner-circleness" about it for members of a particular core of social media spaces, in that it customarily passes between people with a common history or shared interests. Gossip and rumoring in action are recurrent forms of communication in which performers "attempt to construct a meaningful or working interpretation of a threatening or ambiguous situation by polling their intellectual resources" (Tamotsu Shibutani, quoted in Miller 2005, 508) into a group think-tank supported by social media. When the cyber utterances have been gossiped and/or rumored, the narrated text remains attached to the object—evidenced, in this case, through a few undocumented argument essays. It is important to note that these written texts I am remarking on are not subject to plagiarism.

And narrativization goes left as much as it goes right. Born online after the acquittal of George Zimmerman for killing an unarmed black teenager named Trayvon Martin, and translated into the street-level activism after the killing of Michael Brown, the Black Lives Matter movement embodies the belief in the narrated texts, and those texts "stalk" the mainstream community wherever and whenever the movement is perceived as nearby (for the good or the bad of it). Hence, a fear of exclusion and the deployment of #AllLivesMatter are a response. The way we tell stories helps us convey our intended meaning, but how the nonverbal properties of cyber utterances interact with their scripted texts and the recalibrations of already-said texts is a question that is often ignored or not fully addressed.

My first attempt to make sense of the performance and attitude shift in the 2015–2016 school year only examined the texts themselves originally brought to my attention by one of the teaching assistants followed by the other two teaching assistants coming forward. While the tone and expressive choices made by a few students upset my teaching assistants, in particular the African American teaching assistants, the learning outcome reports that I had submitted to the College of Arts and Sciences at the end of the semester revealed something else.

Table 2.1. Learning Outcomes for Short Writing Assignment, 2015–2016

	Number of Students Evaluated	Percentage of Students		
		Below Performance Standard (C– to F)	Meeting Performance Standard (A– to C)	Above Performance Standard (A+ to A)
Fall 2015	255	11%	68%	21%
Spring 2016	252	8%	76%	16%

It is evident that the highest performance standard fell by 5 percent. However, more students had met the overall goal of the assignment and made some improvements in the spring 2016 semester. It is important to note that the two students included in this essay met most of the criteria to obtain grades in the B and C– range.

Given the growing conservatism on campuses that semester and an increasing visibility of alt-right student organizations (for example, Identity Evropa on the IU campus), I anticipated more students for the upcoming 2016–2017 academic year to resist similarly to the students of spring 2016. That did not occur. In fact, more students scored higher overall in both the fall 2016 and spring 2017 semesters.

Table 2.2. Learning Outcomes for Short Writing Assignment, 2015–2016 and 2017

	Number of Students Evaluated	Percentage of Students		
		Below Performance Standard (C– to F)	Meeting Performance Standard (A– to C)	Above Performance Standard (A+ to A)
Fall 2015	255	11%	68%	21%
Spring 2016	252	8%	76%	16%
Fall 2016	251	13%	58%	29%
Spring 2017	235	7%	60%	33%

The teaching assistants for the 2016–2017 academic year were given access to the papers from the previous semesters to serve as models. The interjections for All Lives Matter persisted into the academic year, but mostly as part of a student's concluding thought and typically without an aggressive tone.

Table 2.3. Students' Nonsubmission of the Short Writing Assignment

	Number of Students Performing below the Performance Standard (C– to F)	Number of Students Who Did Not Submit an Essay
Fall 2015	28	18
Spring 2016	31	21
Fall 2016	21	6
Spring 2017	14	8

Another possible place of students resisting the guideline of the short writing assignment could be deduced from the number of students that did not submit an assignment. Arguably, not submitting a paper could be perceived as a space for resistance, especially since the number of students without submissions were more numerous in the second semester than in the first semester of the 2015–2016 academic year. These differences between semesters might also correspond to the higher number of students leaning in favor of the Black Lives Matter movement as well as producing the most vocal protestations against the movement. Furthermore, both traditional media and social media attention shifted heavily toward the race for a Republican candidate and toward the rise of Bernie Sanders's popular following/supporters in January 2016 and away from the ongoing protests led by groups such as BLM and the organizations that have since partnered with BLM, such as the Movement for Black Lives, the Blackout Collective, Mothers against Police Brutality, Alliance for Educational Justice, and Freedom Inc., among others. That period of campaigning witnessed a significant appeal to white working-class and white middle-class voters as a neglected and silent majority and those positions obscured ongoing events that made Mike Brown and Sandra Bland so newsworthy; for example, Gregory Gunn, an unarmed victim who was tased multiple times, beaten with a baton, and shot five times on February 25, 2016, did not become a household name despite the fact that the Alabama police officer who shot him was indicted on a murder charge in November 2016—which is a uncommon event.

I must reiterate that I had anticipated greater resistance to this assignment in the following semesters of the 2016–2017 academic year, but, as I stated above, the aggressive tone was absent and the number of nonsubmissions decreased significantly. It is difficult to determine if the relatively few nonsubmissions were intentional in any of the semesters. In my class, I do not accept late assignments and because it is generally the last essay of the semester, and students already know the standard response from the teaching assistants and me. However, the number of nonsubmissions was drastically lower for the 2016–2017 academic year overall. Even if the students do not agree with BLM, there are data from the lyrics, album covers, or videos that the artists are supporting some elements of the BLM platform.

This assignment asks students to confront current events, contemporary rap music, and national and ethnic relations sociohistorically. My approach attempts to analyze how the students over the two academic years synthesized and interrogated information from the class and then applied them to current events. As the last writing assignment of a class that focuses on the diverse, lived experiences of African American and African-diasporic people and their musical culture, which has been embraced as "American" musical culture, at a minimum, it requires students to grapple with a worldview that might not be their own and that has the potential to couple learning with activism. Ideally, I would have liked to conduct feedback interviews (and perhaps I still will) as time has passed since the first and second semesters. It would be interesting to see whether their attitudes have stayed the same or have changed. I also wonder how best to assess the general agreement of the class each semester that the music is indeed connected to the Black Lives Matter movement. In her 2015 monograph *Pulse of the People*, Lakeyta M. Bonnette argues that political rap serves as a musical method for consciousness raising among African American youth. Her work is thoughtful and self-reflective, recognizing the possibility that "individuals who do listen to political rap may be those who already support Black Nationalist sentiment" (152), and her work took an experimental approach to "uncover causal relationships between exposure to music and responses to political attitudinal questions" (152). Bonnette's book was released at a time during which a new generation of conscious rappers and R&B artists released songs directly addressing the tenets of the Black Live Matter movement and/or the specific cases of murdered black youth, as well as forming artist collectives, such as the West Coast's Black Hippy (Kendrick Lamar, Jay Rock, School-boy Q, and Ab-Soul) or Chicago's SAVEMONEY (Vic Mensa, Chance the Rapper, Donnie Trumpet, and the Social Experiment). Could her thesis include non-African American listeners between 2015 and 2017 who chose to listen to the current trending rappers whose music is rooted in oppositional resistance? Are students of hip hop music culture going beyond hearing the producer's beats and the MC's wordsmithing and listening to the message?

Looking at the results of successfully articulating the connection of an artist's work to the event connected with Black Lives Matter, I propose that the white-supremacist-friendly rhetoric of the 2016 Republican primary season might have emboldened a few students, but the masses were willing to make the connection (even if they did not agree with the activists' ideological and political intervention). We must continue to study how engaging in political hip hop and R&B culture from different communities affects audience members and cultural attitudes.

Conclusion: It Gets Better, but Not Yet . . .

The Black Studies scholar Perry A. Hall contends, "African-American musical sensibilities have profoundly affected mainstream popular culture for over a century. . . . At this and similar points in the history of Black music, it becomes clear that a complex 'love-hate' relationship connects mainstream society and African-American culture" (1997, 31). That is, we fans of black popular music might congratulate ourselves for decolonizing our listening habits, while simultaneously treating the fight for civil rights as a job completed and ignoring or rejecting the contemporary issues that many in the African American community face in this country today.

Ethnomusicologists, folklorists, and anthropologists are trained to aestheticize culture, to live among the people whose ethnographies we write, and, all too often, to leave the suffering of daily life that some of our interlocutors live day in and day out. In the classroom, it is possible to focus too much on artistic expressions and to overlook the important issues relevant to the welfare of the people whose culture we celebrate with our students.

Hip hop has always been a musical and cultural space where artists and fans have engaged in discourses of inequality, homophobia, racism, violence, and misogyny; therefore, implementing critical race theory as an analytic tool in my pedagogy offers an apparatus for my students to consider critical perspectives on race, inequality, the dynamics of political power versus cultural capital, and how we, and all of us have at some point or other, have failed to address the intersectionality of social and cultural domination.

I incorporate hip hop culture to frame issues concerning black cultural artifacts and identity so that students may begin to connect contemporary hip hop artistry with black consciousness and black political culture today. It would be infinitely easier to teach only about style and appeal to race ambivalence and the illusion of a "postracial," Obama millennial population, but I argue that engaging with discourses on class and race interculturally and intraculturally at both conceptual and practical levels expands students' abilities to think through how the complex and multifaceted formations of black consciousness moved from historical contexts beyond a civil rights past (ca. 1950s–1990s) to still resonate today.

My ultimate goal in this chapter is not to make listeners think that dealing with race theory in the classroom should be perceived pessimistically. It is quite the opposite, though my frustration often betrays that sentiment. I urge for optimism because race is a social construction and, therefore, I embrace the idea that it should be subject to ready change, which includes reconciling our own inadvertent acts of microaggression. I began this chapter laying down a context for contemporary racial tensions; in the second half of the essay, I suggest that the activity of writing, like the activity of speaking, is a supremely social act to address the current state of race relations in the United States.

Simultaneously, I believe we shall find that it is far more complex—and therefore more intriguing—than we have suspected before in studying our students' writing ethnographically (Basso [1974] 1989, 432). Most of my students enter the class interested to learn about hip hop song styles and artists, but I aim to encourage them to approach race, gender, social structure, and socioeconomic class in the United States (and beyond) critically, which will serve them to make their corner of the world better. Doing diversity pedagogies in the classroom is not about the rejection of views, the rejection of the white middle-class, or shutting off debate with those who disagree with me; rather it is about achieving a fuller idea regarding pluralism in the US teaching community. Hip hop is one of the most significant contributions to the Black Lives Matter movement's soundscape and pretending that hip hop studies is not about black political culture is itself a loud, political statement.

NOTES

1. I am indebted to Richard Bauman for sharing *Student Writing and Genre* and other resources for this essay.

2. The full video is difficult to locate on most video-sharing websites. Some clips resurface in news reports. My first viewing led me to believe that it was a parody done in poor taste. After watching the video several times, I realized that the song was not tongue-in-cheek and that the rapper might truly be unaware of the fact that she is appropriating a black music form to express her racist viewpoints. See *Washington Post*, February 22, 2017, for the report (https://www.washingtonpost.com/news/grade-point/wp/2017/02/22/we-are-sickened-by-this-old-dominion-investigates-video-promoting-lynching-and-white-power/?utm_term=.a3486ad76854).

3. The alt-right banner appropriated the idea of anarchic "punk" behavior and punk rock but with far-right ideologies. The spirit of punk is typically associated with left-wing, anti-authoritarianism; hence, alternative, noncommercial hard rock. The new alternative is one that embraces the raucous attitude and supports a right-wing authoritarianism. Alt-right public speakers such as Milo Yiannopoulos have been invited by students to speak on traditionally liberal campuses across the country.

4. Here, I reference André Jolles's use of the term "superorganic" to refer to simple forms (legends, saga, myths, riddles, fairytales, cases, sayings, memorabilia, and jokes) as their formation by human agents is less significant to their existence as communicative text. Treating verbal art forms this way, and I include song and lyrics for our purposes, is problematic because it makes them autonomous, and it does not require reference to social or cultural conditions to explain meaning, function, or how they are situated in an emergent performative event.

WORKS CITED

Basso, Keith. (1974) 1989. "The Ethnography of Writing." In *Explorations in the Ethnography of Speaking*, 2nd ed., edited by Richard Bauman and Joel Sherzer, 425–432. New York: Cambridge University Press.

Bauman, Richard. 2004. *A World of Others' Words: Cross-Cultural Perspectives on Intertextuality*. Malden, MA: Blackwell.

Bonnette, Lakeyta M. 2015. *Pulse of the People: Political Rap Music and Black Politics*. Philadelphia: University of Pennsylvania Press.

Delgado, Richard, and Jean Stefancic, eds. 2012. *Critical Race Theory: An Introduction*. New York: New York University Press.

English, Fiona. 2011. *Student Writing and Genre: Reconfiguring Academic Knowledge*. New York: Continuum.

Fludernik, Monika. (1996) 2010. *Towards a "Natural" Narratology.* New York: Rout-
    ledge.
Garza, Alicia. 2014. "A Herstory of the #BlackLivesMatter Movement." *The Feminist
    Wire,* October 7, 2014. http://www.thefeministwire.com/2014/10/blacklives
    matter-2/.
Hall, Perry A. 1997. "African-American Music: Dynamics of Appropriation and Innova-
    tion." In *Borrowed Power: Essays on Cultural Appropriation,* edited by Bruce H. Ziff
    and Pratima V. Rao, 30–51. New Brunswick, NJ: Rutgers University Press.
Jackson, Noel. 2013. "Of Borrowed Words on Social Media." https://noelbjackson
    .wordpress.com/2013/11/22/366/.
Jolles, André. *Simple Forms [Einfache Formen].* 2017. Translated by Peter J. Schwartz.
    Foreword by Fredric Jameson. Brooklyn, NY: Verso.
Lanich, Carley. 2015. "IUPD Investigating Racist Comments Made on Social Media."
    Indiana Daily Student, November 13, 2015. http://www.idsnews.com/article
    /2015/11/iupd-investigating-racist-comments-made-on-social-media.
Lomborg, Stine. 2013. *Social Media, Social Genres.* New York: Routledge.
Miller, Dan E. 2005. "Rumor: An Examination of Some Stereotypes." *Symbolic Interac-
    tion* 28 (4): 505–519.
Phillips, Chuck. 1992. "The Uncivil War: The Battle between the Establishment and Sup-
    porters of Rap Music Reopens Old Wounds of Race and Class." *Los Angeles Times,*
    July 19, 1992.
Rosnow, R. L. 2001. "Rumor and Gossip in Interpersonal Interaction and Beyond: A So-
    cial Exchange Perspective." In *Behaving Badly: Aversive Behaviors in Interpersonal
    Relationships,* edited by R. M. Kowalski, 203–232. Washington, DC: American
    Psychological Association.
University Institutional Research and Reporting. 2016. "Student Diversity." https://uirr
    .iu.edu/facts-figures/enrollment/diversity/index.html.
Wortham, Stanton, and Angela Reyes. 2014. *Discourse Analysis beyond the Speech Event.*
    New York: Routledge.

FERNANDO OREJUELA is Senior Lecturer and Director of Undergraduate Studies in the Department of Folklore and Ethnomusicology at
Indiana University. He is author of *Rap Music and Hip Hop Culture.*

THREE

BLACK FOLKLIFE MATTERS: SLABS AND THE SOCIAL IMPORTANCE OF CONTEMPORARY AFRICAN AMERICAN FOLKLIFE

Langston Collin Wilkins

ON SATURDAY AFTERNOON, OCTOBER 20, 2013, nearly four thousand people gathered in Houston's iconic MacGregor Park to experience an event: the first Houston SLAB Parade and Family festival. The event was a celebration of SLAB, a vernacular vehicle culture that developed among working-class African American men in the mid-1980s in Houston, Texas. SLABs are outmoded American luxury-brand vehicles that are customized in candy colors and adorned with various types of embellishments. The parade began with a fifty-car processional into the park. A single line of cars drove into the park at a sluggish pace, aided only by the mishmash of hip hop sounds coming from their powerful stereo systems. On the northwest corner of the park, a reserved section was laid out for the cars to situate themselves in an orderly, color-coded fashion. Reflecting a core practice within the SLAB community, there were sections for red cars, blue cars, green cars, teal cars, gold cars, and cars of other assorted colors. A minifestival followed the parade. Local hip hop artists such as E.S.G., the Bloc Boyz Click, K-Rino, and Yungstar performed. Dance teams and poets also performed while local vendors promoted and sold their products and services.

In the age of Black Lives Matter, a wide range of speculation and scholarship has attempted to analyze and contextualize black experiences in order to help illuminate the state of race relations in twenty-first-century America.

This approach informed my doctoral dissertation research, which examined how artists' attachment to their neighborhoods is reflected in their musical output by way of a homegrown brand of hip hop music, screwed music, also known as screwed and chopped. While my ethnomusicological research focused on the screwed music scene, I quickly became intrigued by SLAB culture, and I recognized that it was an inseparable, visual art product of the same scene and, thus, reflects the Black Lives Matter platform by being a sustainable cultural component that is unapologetically black, cultivates community, and promotes self-definition and self-sufficiency

Further, the parade's meaning went well beyond pure spectacle. It reflected the social benefits of a critical engagement with African American folklife. Conducting research into SLAB culture and planning the Houston SLAB Parade and Family Festival helped me recognize the need for increased attention to contemporary African American folklife. In this chapter, I use SLAB culture as a case study to examine identity formation and community-building efforts within African American folk scenes and to argue that programming around local forms of African American folk music and folklife can help dismantle destructive stereotypes that victimize and vilify African Americans and help make the social narrative of a place more culturally pluralistic.

What Is a SLAB?

SLABs are not mass-produced. They are custom made over the course of several months or years and can cost thousands of dollars to complete. SLAB owners often do some of their own customization, but they also employ community artisans that specialize in particular components. For example, SLAB owners B.G. and Meyagi are popular customizers who specialize in body and interior work. China Boy is an audio system designer and installer. Most SLAB customizers are either self-taught or they learn their respective trades from elders in the community. Ultimately, like all folk arts, a finished SLAB is the result of both individual and communal development.

The most important aesthetic components of a SLAB are the "swangas," chrome rims that feature spokes protruding from the base in the shape of a cone. There are two types of swangas and both were originally rims that Crager Wheel Company produced for Cadillac models in the early 1980s: the "83s" and the "84s." The 83s were produced for Cadillac El Dorado models

Figure 3.1 SLABs during a SLAB holiday. Galveston, Texas. May 19, 2012. Photo by author.

Figure 3.2 An 84-style swanga at the Action Smoke Shop block party. Houston, Texas. May 27, 2012. Photo by author.

beginning in 1979 and ending in 1983. The more popular 84s are a modified version of the 83s. The 84s featured a reduced lip, more space between the outer ten spokes, and the spokes poke out much further than the 83s. The look is complete with a core SLAB component, Vogues, a tire marked by its distinctive whitewall and yellow stripe. Vogues are also common to other car-culture scenes in the American South.

The "grille and woman" make up the front end of a SLAB vehicle. The chrome grille is a common sedan component that covers an opening in the front end that allows air to enter the engine. The "woman" refers to a goddess-type hood ornament that sits on top of the hood. The rear of the SLAB is carefully crafted with a "fifth wheel," which, in essence, is a decorative spare tire in the swanga style that is cut in half and enclosed in a fiberglass case. It is attached to the trunk with a chrome device called a "bumper kit." SLABs are also marked by their vibrant exterior paint jobs, commonly called "candy paint." Local customizers use iridescent paint to give the cars a very "wet" appearance when hit by light. Finally, SLABs are also outfitted with explosive sound systems that are powered by several speakers and twelve- to fifteen-inch subwoofers.

The origin of the term "SLAB" is rooted in oral tradition and has two popular threads, both pointing to the concrete slabs that compose the typical American street. A few of my interlocutors told me that these particular types of custom vehicles became known as SLABs because of their lengthy creation process. SLABs, both in their infancy and today, can take several weeks or years to complete due to labor. When the cars were finished and ready to be presented, early SLAB riders would say, "I'm about to hit the slab," or something similar. Other interlocutors contend that people began calling the vehicles SLABs because the addition of many foreign components of the cars weighed them down, making the car sit lower to the concrete "slabs" of the street. In the 1990s, SLAB turned to an acronym that stands for "slow, loud, and bangin'." The origins of the acronym are unknown, but it is closely associated with rap group S.L.A.B., a crew of MCs helmed by popular local rap artists Z-Ro and Trae That Truth. While the acronym-based spelling is sometimes used, it is more common for SLAB to be capitalized without the periods as I do throughout this essay. The reasons behind this, like other aspects of the culture, are lost to history

History of SLAB Culture

The story of SLAB begins in the Southside, a colloquialism for the collective of interconnected African American neighborhoods situated southeast of downtown Houston.

In the mid-1980s, the Southside was in the midst of the crack era, with young men feeling disenfranchised and excluded from economic and higher education opportunities, leading them to opt for alternative financial avenues. Some were getting rich peddling crack within their neighborhood. Scott, one such Southside drug dealer, told me that he earned upward of $2,500 a night dealing drugs right out of his garage (O.G. Scott, interview with the author, March 2012). With all of these excess funds, the Southside streets became locations of displays of vanity. Customizing a SLAB become one of the foremost ways that local drug dealers could mark their economic success. The decorative, chrome 84 swangas became the most important SLAB component in this respect. Cadillac deemed them a road hazard and they were only produced for a single year, which made them extremely rare. Their exclusivity rendered them highly popular and valuable on the Southside streets. The swangas solidified the culture and additional body components and related practices emerged over time.

In the mid-1990s, the SLAB scene and the local hip hop scene became inextricably linked, fused together by artists who were as deep in the streets as they were in the rap game. The Screwed Up Click, a Southside-based rap crew, were central forces in this cultural fusion. The foundation of the Screwed Up Click was DJ Screw, a Southside resident, who developed Houston's sonic identity by creating slow, psychedelic mixes called "screwtapes" that were inspired by Houston's unhurried atmosphere. Joining DJ Screw in the Screwed Up Click were a collective of street hustlers and street hustlers-turned-MCs from the Southside, some of whom performed freestyles that offered stream-of-consciousness views of Southside street life. As the Screwed Up Click organically emerged out of local street culture, its constitution became inscribed with SLAB life. Screwed Up Click member E.S.G. notes that "the reason why the niggas was talkin' about the SLABs and shit was because these was the niggas [SLAB riders] goin' to Screw's house makin' the screwtapes" (E.S.G., interview with the author, March

2012). Southside SLAB riders like Corey Blunt, C-Note, Stick-1, and Fat Pat became the Screwed Up Click's earliest members.

E.S.G.'s "Swangin' n Bangin'" (1994) is widely considered to be the earliest musical documentation of and dedication to the Southside SLAB scene. Born Cedric Hill in Bogalusa, Louisiana, E.S.G. moved to the Southside as a teenager. At the time, according to E.S.G, "The southside was playa." So E.S.G. sought to record a song that "included everything pertaining to the culture and place we were living in" (E.S.G., interview with the author, March 2012). Produced by Sean Solo Jemison, "Swangin' n Bangin'" offers a vivid description of the SLAB scene. The title and chorus, "Swangin' n Bangin'," refers to the practices of swangin', which involves driving at an extremely low speed, weaving from lane to lane, and bangin', which is playing the car's stereo at a high volume in order to sonically announce one's presence. Throughout the song, E.S.G. details core elements of SLAB aesthetics, including 84s, Vogue tires, bubble headlights, fifth wheels, grilles, and candy-color paint. The immense popularity of "Swangin' n Bangin'" and later SLAB anthems like Big Mello's "Wegonfunkwichamind" (1994), Fat Pat's "Tops Drop" (1998), and Mike Jones's "Still Tippin'" (2004) helped cement SLAB as a core part of Houston hip hop identity both in and outside of Houston.

SLAB's Significance for Community Members

While conducting my ethnomusicological dissertation research, my early attempts to engage with the SLAB scene were unsuccessful. I approached quite a few SLAB owners at various events around town. I asked them about their cars, explained the source of my interest, and gave them my business card in case they were interested in talking to me about the culture. No one responded. I had promising interactions with a SLAB rider from Houston's Hiram Clarke neighborhood, but even that proved futile because he would not commit to meeting. I learned that SLAB culture was much more difficult to access and navigate than the hip hop scene. Unlike rap artists, who are looking to promote themselves and their music to the widest audience possible, SLAB riders generally keep a low profile. SLAB is an insular street-based culture and its participants are often hesitant to interact with outsiders.

At the very moment I was about to give up on this venture and revert my attention back to music, I came upon a music video called "Officially Ridin' Swings" by a local rap group called the Bloc Boyz Click. The song and video are dedicated to SLAB culture in Houston. Released in 2009, the video is a SLAB anthem of sorts as it features vivid lyrical and visual references to SLAB culture. I searched the internet for contact information for the Bloc Boyz Click and found their manager's Facebook page. I sent him a Facebook message explaining who I was as well as the details of my project. Thankfully, he responded and put me in touch with O.G. Scott, the owner of the Bloc Boyz Click's record label, Blackhouse Records. O.G. Scott invited me to his home in the Cloverland neighborhood in Houston's Southside, where, on a cool March evening in 2012, I met the members of the Bloc Boyz Click as well as various SLAB riders whom O.G. Scott had convened. O.G. Scott and the Bloc Boyz Click became my guides into the SLAB scene. The group provided foundational information about SLABs, actively informed me about SLAB events, and connected me with other notable figures within the culture.

As I became more invested in my SLAB culture research, the community was still reeling from a violent incident that had occurred two years earlier. On March 21, 2010, three-year-old Charissa Powell was shot and killed by Alton Charles Barnes during an attempted carjacking on Houston's Northside. Charles Powell, Charissa's father, was getting his kids strapped into the car, when Barnes walked up to him and demanded his keys. Recognizing the danger, Powell attempted to get his kids out of the car. That is when Barnes allegedly began firing his AK-47 into the car. Barnes's bullets hit Powell in the chest, killing her. Investigators believed that Barnes was attempting to steal the "swangas" off her father's blue Pontiac SLAB. Charles Powell agrees. "He shot her in the process of trying to shoot me, to rob for some 'swangers,'" he says. "If I knew that, I would have never taken my kids outside" (ABC13 News 2010). Powell's early death was the latest in a legacy of violence that has long plagued the SLAB community. SLAB's expensive modifications, especially the swangas, have long attracted carjackers seeking a quick financial windfall. Again, SLAB riders operate in communities plagued by poverty. SLABs are, unfortunately, very accessible means of making quick cash on the black market. Violence in the community peaked in the mid-1990s when the swangas were in short supply and cost nearly $10,000 for a set of four. Texan Wire Wheels, a California-based company, relieved much of the violence when they began mass-manufacturing the rims in the 2000s, which brought costs down. Powell's death, however, reminded them that despite their best efforts, the specters of violence always loomed.

Violence is problematic, and I quickly learned that the vibrant vernacular art form and culture, with a wide variety of meanings for its participants, helped sublimate that problem. SLABs are born out of individual ingenuity and a strong sense of community. To the former, SLAB riders seek to use the cars as extensions of their personal identity. Every component of the car is inscribed with its owner's ideas and experiences. However, community is a key part of SLAB practice and this can be witnessed on the bodies of the cars as well as the particular ways that they operate. As previously mentioned, SLABs commonly feature two- and three-dimensional trunk displays that often serve as memorials to places and people. These trunk displays make explicit references to predominantly African American neighborhoods such as Trinity Gardens, Forth Ward, and Fontaine. They also feature lettered or graphic tributes to deceased loved ones from these communities. Relatedly, SLAB lines are another core practice. These are informal car clubs based on paint color that typically represent particular Houston neighborhoods. These SLAB lines proceed into events in a line, position themselves together, and exit events in the same manner. Their goal is to show community togetherness and strength.

SLABs also reveal the presence of a unique subculture within Houston's black working-class communities that my interlocutors call "the streets." This subculture is generated out of the poverty, joblessness, and disenfranchisement within Houston's black communities. Oppressed and isolated, those within the street have chosen to largely reshape or outright reject tenets of mainstream culture and live according to their own ideals. SLAB's function as a marker of power reflects this rejection. New luxury and sports cars are preeminent status symbols within Houston's predominantly white cultural mainstream. Their high price tags make them exclusive, and ownership signifies the accumulation of a significant amount of material wealth. As such, owning a Lexus, BMW, or Mercedes-Benz can generate much cultural capital; however, these cars do not have the same level of importance within Houston's black street culture. Instead, SLABs are the preeminent vehicle-based form of cultural capital on the streets. SLABs are similar to high-end, luxury vehicles in that they symbolize material wealth, yet their function as capital go beyond their mere cost to own. Possession of a SLAB suggests that its owner has the proper aesthetic knowledge, a high connection to community, and an adequate ability to protect himself from violent threats. SLABs are the ultimate status symbol and represent the community's desire for self-definition and self-sufficiency.

Houston SLAB Parade and Family Festival

SLAB culture occupied a marginal position outside of Houston's African American neighborhoods, despite its long and influential history. Its marginalization was peculiar, considering the importance of cars in local identity and culture. Various vehicle cultures and practices developed in the city during the twentieth century and are still active today. It is very common to see lifted trucks, muscle cars, and customized motorbikes traverse the city's vast expanse. Reflecting the prominence of car culture in the city, the more elaborately customized vehicles are featured in the legendary Houston Art Car Parade. Founded in 1988, the Houston Art Car Parade is a three-day event centered around a parade that features nearly 250 customized vehicles. The parade includes a contest with several different categories. There are categories for more traditional custom vehicles such as low riders, performance vehicles, and motorcycles. However, the Art Car Parade also features many unconventional entries. For example, the 2016 winners included a vehicle tribute to Queen that included a life-size statue of Freddy Mercury attached to the top and a car shaped like Yoda, the beloved character from the *Star Wars* films. While the event features submissions from both laypersons and artists from all over the country, most entries come from the city itself. SLABs, however, were still not included in the Art Car Parade in my time conducting fieldwork. This fact remains true, despite SLAB being a homegrown culture and being nearly thirty years old. It was possible that the SLAB community had no interest in the Art Car Parade. However, I suspected that the absence of SLABs had more to do with the relative isolation of the black working-class experience in general.

SLAB culture's marginalization troubled me. The culture is homegrown, intergenerational, and influential, having spread outside of Houston to other places such as Austin, Texas; Baton Rouge, Louisiana; and Little Rock, Arkansas. Yet it was on the periphery of Houston's cultural landscape. Seeking to raise SLAB's profile, I began to think of ways to present the culture on a large scale. A parade seemed like the most logical and effective endeavor because the processional was already a core practice within the community. I first brought the idea of the parade to members of the Bloc Boyz Click. They were my primary connection to the SLAB community, and I felt that they would be able to gauge the SLAB community's interest in such an event. It was important for me to first present the idea to the SLAB community because, ultimately, I wanted the parade to benefit them. Participants in SLAB culture constantly hold informal parades and car shows and may not have seen the value in it, or they may have been totally averse to it, preferring their established insularity and isolation. O.G. Scott, and subsequently others in the Bloc Boyz Click, calmed my concerns and suggested that a parade would have the full support of the SLAB community.

After getting support from the Bloc Boyz Click, I brought the idea to two local cultural organizations: The Houston Arts Alliance and the Houston Museum of African American Culture. In 2011–2012, I held a joint fellowship with the two organizations where I conducted fieldwork within various African diasporic communities in the city. My fieldwork ultimately resulted in two public programs on the dress and religious music of local African American, Ethiopian, Garifuna, Nigerian, and Cameroonian communities. While my fellowship work was far removed from my interest in SLAB, I suspected that the two organizations would be open to the SLAB parade because both showed an interest in working with the local hip hop scene.

Despite the involvement of two cultural institutions, the parade would not have been a success without the active assistance of the SLAB community throughout the planning process. The Bloc Boyz Click recruited Fourth Ward Fish, who calls himself the SLAB King because of his collection of fully customized SLABs, to help with the event. Fish, in turn, recruited Paul Wall, one of Houston's most popular and mainstream rap artists and a participant in the SLAB community. The Bloc Boyz Click, Paul Wall, and Fourth Ward Fish helped recruit and register parade participants, procure performers for the festival portion, and market the event. The presence of members of the SLAB and hip hop communities on the planning team was vital to the parade's success. SLAB riders are typically averse to

Figure 3.3 A line of SLABs at the Houston SLAB Parade and Family Festival. October 20, 2013. Photo by author.

the bureaucratic institutions and processes involved in the staging of a city-sanctioned event. Their concerns are understandable, considering that they often feel the weight of bureaucratic oppression. Including the community in the planning helped bring transparency to the process, calming any fears about the purpose of the event or any threats to their livelihood that may come from it. This approach allowed the community to retain ownership and control while, at the same time, accessing the resources and infrastructure of these civic institutions.

The SLAB community also helped bring a sense of authenticity to the event. They were instrumental in shaping the event into something that would have much meaning and value for participants. Our goal was not to simply translate or sanitize the culture for outsiders. Rather, we wanted to recognize and celebrate SLAB as a culturally important vernacular art form and practice, while also offering the audience an educational, enriching, and stimulating look into the practice. The event location, MacGregor Park, reflects our goals. MacGregor Park rests at the northern border of the predominantly African American neighborhood of South Park, a longtime hotbed of SLAB activity. From the 1980s to now, it has been normal to see informal SLAB processionals traverse neighborhood streets, most notably Martin Luther King Blvd. MacGregor Park is a popular SLAB gathering place. It is a large park with giant parking lots, making it a prime spot to display SLABs while socializing. We considered other locations, most notably Discovery Green Park in downtown Houston, but felt that centering the event at MacGregor Park would be much truer to SLAB culture. In addition, we felt that holding the event in South Park would, at least for a moment, disrupt the de facto segregation that spatially divides the city. We hoped to bring a cross-section of Houstonians into the mainly black South Park in order to celebrate a distinctly black art form.

The planning committee included a cross-section of Houston-based individuals and institutions. However, the parade did not garner the support of all Houstonians. The parade received some significant pushback from residents of the upper middle-class African American neighborhood that occupies MacGregor Park's western border. Revealing the class politics at play in African American communities, members of this community did not see the social value in the event and did not want their neighborhood to be associated with what they deemed to be an illicit practice. Further, playing into unfortunate stereotypes, they worried that the event would bring violence into the area. We were able to calm some of their concerns through a series of meetings at the area sheriff's office, where we discussed the importance of the event, logistics, and our security plan. Support from the sheriff as well as Houston City Council District D, who eventually became a cosponsor, helped that particular community feel more at ease with the event.

In the wake of the SLAB parade, SLAB has taken on a larger space in Houston's cultural landscape. In late 2013, Houston-born pop superstar Beyoncé featured SLABs and footage from the SLAB parade in the music video for the song "No Angel" from her eponymous 2013 visual album. In 2015, the Travel Channel's *Booze Traveler*, an alcoholic beverage-focused travel show, featured SLAB culture in its segment about Houston. The show host, Jack Maxwell, rode in a SLAB belonging to Houstonian and longtime SLAB rider P Izm during his tour of Houston. Similarly, in 2016 CNN's *Anthony Bourdain: Parts Unknown* included SLAB in its profile of Houston culture.

The most important effects of the SLAB parade were felt in Houston. Most notably, Anise Parker, a former Houston mayor, even rode in a SLAB during the 2015 Art Car Parade. As previously noted, the Houston Art Car parade had never featured SLABs in its twenty-seven-year history, despite the fact that SLABs are, by definition, art cars. The Art Car Parade even created a contest category for SLABs, solidifying its place in the event. SLAB's inclusion in the parade, along with the mayor riding in one, reflects its movement from the margins to the mainstream. Thus, black working-class cultural expression is being integrated into Houston's cultural fabric.

CONCLUSION

The dominantly working-class African American males of the SLAB community face hindrances to their economic and social mobility that are rooted in and shaped by systemic oppression. Nationally, African American men are unemployed at a rate that is double that of their white, Asian, and Hispanic counterparts (Witters and Liu 2015). Incarceration rates are at alarming levels. Black men are six times more likely to be incarcerated than their white counterparts (Drake 2013). Similarly, violent crime rates are at epidemic proportions. Black men are nearly twelve times more likely to die from homicides than white people (Devaney 2016), and homicide is the leading cause of death for those between the ages of fifteen and thirty-four (Centers for Disease Control and Prevention 2014). Black men have been reduced to pathological stereotypes, criminal aggressors to be feared or rendered flat and "othered." This dehumanization has implications for their social life, educational success, and engagement with the criminal justice system.

Black Lives Matter is a national, decentralized movement against such aforementioned antiblack oppression. The organization has worked to counter the dehumanization of African Americans that far too often results in police violence against black men and women. Multidimensional in nature, members of the movement combine explicitly political measures such as rallies, marches, and policy with curriculum, literature, and art to mobilize a critical resistance. As a folk art form and social practice, SLAB reflects core Black Lives Matter principles as its participants celebrate diversity, are unapologetically black, and champion self-definition and self-sufficiency. While the culture can certainly do more to make space for female and LGBTQ+ participants, SLAB remains a good example of the political resistance inherent in everyday African American folk music and practices.

Affirming black lives and valuing diversity, core principles of Black Lives Matter's paradigm, were key motives for my creation of the Houston SLAB Parade and Family Festival. Through the parade, I sought to create a public space for an unapologetic affirmation and celebration of blackness. I wanted the SLAB community actively involved in the planning process in order to prevent the possibility of misrepresentation or cultural whitewashing. The parade was able to reshape Houston's cultural narrative, making it much more pluralistic. It has helped mitigate feelings of social isolation, and it made the black working-class experience part of Houston's identity, rather than an unfortunate by-product. While such endeavors cannot solve America's "race problem," I feel that my critical engagement with SLAB has helped produce a counternarrative of the lives of black working-class men, one that humanizes rather than demonizes, and I push for a similar investment in other folk forms across the United States. The Black Lives Matter platform is multidimensional and makes it a point to include black women and members of the LGBTQ+ community at the center of its work. Both groups are largely excluded from the SLAB community in a very problematic way. Even with such faults, SLAB is a good example of the community-based activism that is a central component of Black Lives Matter's pathway to liberation.

Works Cited

ABC13 News. 2010. "Father of Girl Killed in Carjacking Attempt Speaks." March 26, 2010. http://abc13.com/archive/7351877/

Centers for Disease Control and Prevention. 2014. "Leading Causes of Death (LCOD) by Age Group, Black Males—United States, 2014." Accessed March 12, 2017. https://www.cdc.gov/healthequity/lcod/men/2014/black/index.htm.

Devaney, Tim. 2016. "FBI: Black Men 12 Times More Likely to Be Murdered Than White People." *The Hill,* March 3, 2016. http://thehill.com/regulation/271630-fbi -black-men-12-times-more-likely-to-be-murdered-than-white-people.

Drake, Bruce. 2013. "Incarceration Gap Widens between Whites and Blacks." *Pew Research Center,* September 6, 2013. http://www.pewresearch.org/fact-tank/2013/09 /06/incarceration-gap-between-whites-and-blacks-widens/.

Witters, Dan, and Diana Liu. 2015. "Young Black Males' Well-Being Harmed More by Unemployment." *Gallup.com*. April 23, 2015. http://www.gallup.com/poll/182507/young-black-males-harmed-unemployment.aspx

LANGSTON COLLIN WILKINS is Traditional Arts Specialist with the Tennessee Arts Commission. He is currently writing an ethnographic manuscript on the cultivation of local identity within Houston's screwed and chopped hip hop music scene.

FOUR

BLACK MUSIC MATTERS: AFFIRMATION AND RESILIENCE IN AFRICAN AMERICAN MUSICAL SPACES IN WASHINGTON, DC

Alison Martin

As an ethnomusicologist working within the soundscapes of nightlife, I spend a considerable amount of time in nightclubs, scrolling through social media on my phone. On one such night in the summer of 2016, I was scrolling through Twitter and saw several videos made by black protesters in Baton Rouge, Louisiana, running from police officers in riot gear. This particular night was July 8, three days after the murder of Alton Sterling by a police officer in Baton Rouge and two days after the murder of Philando Castile by a police officer in Falcon Heights, Minnesota.[1] Meanwhile, in the DC club in which I was conducting fieldwork, the SOS go-go band was performing a cover of Beyoncé's "Freedom," a hard-hitting anthem featuring Kendrick Lamar, whose music has become an unofficial soundtrack to the Black Lives Matter movement. It was in this moment that I started to think about go-go music, a subgenre of funk local to Washington, DC, as connected to the activism and narratives I was witnessing online and all over the country.

In this chapter, I argue that the musical and expressive practices within the go-go music community of DC exemplifies the core ideals of the Black Lives Matter movement, or BLM, as outlined by Alicia Garza, one of the co-founders of the movement. In providing a "herstory" of the movement, Garza argues that Black Lives Matter is "an affirmation of Black folks' contributions to this society, our humanity, and our resilience in the face of deadly oppression" (Garza 2014). While there are other explanations of the movement, I take this definition from one of the founders as my starting point in understanding the connection between go-go and Black Lives Matter. Utilizing examples from fieldwork I conducted in DC in 2016, I argue that go-go both affirms the humanity of the black community of DC and is resilient in the face of both local and national systems of oppression. In doing so, I use this chapter to envision the go-go community in an activist light, situating them within a larger genealogy of black musical resistance. Black music has, for centuries, been a tool through which communities both affirm life and exert resilience against forces of oppression. I also want to consider a discussion of politicized ethnomusicology, considering not only my role as an ethnomusicologist but also the emotional labor of working on Black Lives Matter as a black woman.

Within the discipline of ethnomusicology, Philip Bohlman has been very vocal about the necessity of political scholarship, arguing that "an apolitical ethnomusicology is also an ahistorical ethnomusicology, which itself can only be a construction of a scholarship that believes it can turn its back to the intervention of history" (2008, 109). Furthermore, he advocates for contemporary politics as an effective framework for ethnomusicology. This chapter attempts to follow the two edicts, drawing both on the racialized history of DC but also considering the contemporary moment that we find ourselves in, between both the Black Lives Matter movement and the Trump administration.

My scholarship must be political, public, and even activist in nature. I am committed to the decriminalization of black bodies, taking care to emphasize that this includes my own black body. My politics involve acknowledging my own emotional labor, and seeking emotional justice not only for myself but also for the communities that suffer from the proximity to death that comes from being a black person in DC (and in this country). Emotional justice, coined by radio host Esther Armah, refers to "the remedy for the legacy of untreated trauma impacting us as a people" (2012). Within my work, I seek emotional justice through my efforts to humanize black musical gathering spaces.

My contribution to this volume is, in part, the result of the ethnography and musical analysis of go-go music that I proposed for my dissertation. In this chapter, though, I draw on the musical and expressive practices of the go-go music community as a point of entry to explore the politics of black musical affirmation and resilience. I include my own experiences as an ethnographer and as a black woman in order to help readers understand what it means to be black and vulnerable, to be black and expendable, to be black and in danger. Go-go puts to practice the ideals of the Black Lives Matter movement and this, to me, is crucial because it is through scenes like go-go music that black people are able to make a way out of no way.

Black Lives Matter

Black Lives Matter began on July 13, 2013, as a response to the acquittal of George Zimmerman for the murder of the unarmed black teenager Trayvon Martin in Sanford, Florida, on February 26, 2012. Zimmerman, a resident of the neighborhood in which Martin's father resided, followed the teenager as he walked home, calling the police to report that "this guy looks like he's up to no good. . . . Something's wrong with him. . . . He's got something in his hands" (*Washington Post* 2012). Although instructed to wait for the police and not follow the teenager, Zimmerman continued to stalk Martin, shooting and killing him after a violent confrontation. The seventeen-year-old had been carrying a can of iced tea and a pack of Skittles.

Since Zimmerman's acquittal for the murder of Trayvon Martin, there has been a renewed mobilization around antiblack racism in the United States, revolving particularly around issues of police brutality. Black people are routinely stopped and harassed by police across the country at rates much higher than white people. These stops often result in unlawful arrests and, too often, in death (Lowery 2015). Outrage and grief surrounding the premature death of black people at the hands of the police (and also at the hands of civilians, such as George Zimmerman) led to the creation of this massive movement. Founded by Opal Tometi, Alicia Garza, and Patrisse Cullors, Black Lives Matter has changed the ways in which people in the United States engage in conversations about race (specifically blackness) and with the police.

Social media is one of the tools that has propelled Black Lives Matter to the level of visibility it has today. The names of slain black people have become hashtags, which in turn become rallying cries for protesters and others who consider themselves participants in this movement. Popular phrases trending in 2015–2016 include #sayhername, which specifically acknowledges police brutality against black women, and #Icantbreathe, which references the dying words of Eric Garner, who was choked to death by a New York Police Department officer, Daniel Pantaleo.[2]

Black Lives Matter is larger than the activism against police brutality. Organizers are also focused on environmental justice (particularly in Flint, Michigan), criminal justice reform, and black political participation.[3] In August 2016, the Movement for Black Lives released a political platform, "A Vision for Black Lives," outlining their demands as well as the legislative measures that they wish to take to realize these demands. The platform features six areas of action: ending the war on black people, reparations, invest-divest, economic justice, community control, and political power. As the Movement for Black Lives operates intentionally with no central leader, this platform is the collaborative effort of a staggering number of individuals and organizations committed to bettering the lives of black people.

Historian Robin D. G. Kelley offered an insightful analysis of this platform, arguing that it is "less a political platform than a plan for ending structural racism, saving the planet, and transforming the entire nation—not just black lives" (2016, 5). Indeed, the platform is holistic, attentive to the African diaspora, and centers the needs of the most marginalized of an already marginalized community, specifically "women, queer, trans, femmes, gender nonconforming, Muslim, formerly and currently incarcerated, cash poor and working class, disabled, undocumented, and immigrant" (Movement for Black Lives 2016). The platform argues that "there can be no liberation for all Black people if we do not center and fight for those who have been marginalized" (2016). I read this platform as expanding on and uplifting the words of Alicia Garza regarding the affirmation of black life and persistent struggle against state violence. Focused specifically on policy reform, the platform speaks to solidarity within the black community and within a larger framework of oppressed peoples, and it also recognizes the fact that "black people have bravely and brilliantly been the driving force pushing the U.S. towards the ideals it articulates but has never achieved" (2016).

Even amid the specificity and intentionality of this platform, the Black Lives Matter movement has been derided as antipolice, antiwhite, and, particularly because of Colin Kaepernick's 2016 NFL protest during the national anthem, as anti-American. In some spaces, Black Lives Matter has even been characterized as a hate group or terrorist organization.[4] I argue that the movement is perceived in this way because it rejects racial color-blindness as a goal. Instead, it holds the state accountable for its systemic racism and violence, systems that have a large presence in the nation's capital.

Establishing the Chocolate City

Like the nation itself, Washington, DC, has been fraught with the ramifications of racism since its inception. Established in 1790 and designed by the French architect Pierre L'Enfant, the city was built on land ceded by Maryland and Virginia, two slave states (Gillette 2011). The federal city was a slaveholding city, and it remained as such until enslaved persons were emancipated in DC on April 16, 1862, almost nine months before Abraham Lincoln signed the Emancipation Proclamation on January 1, 1863. Enslaved persons were able to be freed before the rest of those in the nation because Congress retains executive power over the city.

By 1900, the African American population in DC had grown in such a way that the city held the highest percentage of African Americans in the country (McQuirter 2003). People came for a myriad of reasons, particularly for educational opportunities as well as federal government jobs.[5] Migration to DC continued throughout the Great Migration of the early twentieth century. DC became home for a growing black cultural elite, and the U Street Corridor, known as "Black Broadway," thrived from the 1920s through the 1960s. While many members of the black community in DC were flourishing, the city remained segregated, partially through the use of restrictive racial housing covenants. These covenants, some by deed and some by petition, restricted who could live in certain houses. The residue of these covenants is one of the reasons why the northwestern area of the city remains primarily white. Urban renewal and previous waves of gentrification have also contributed to the segregation within the city (Asch and Musgrove 2016).

DC was an active center of the civil rights movement, famously hosting the March for Jobs and Freedom in 1963. After the assassination of Dr. Martin Luther King Jr. in 1968, riots overtook the city, and prominent black neighborhoods were burned. These neighborhoods included cultural landmarks of the U Street Corridor and the H Street Corridor. Amid this unrest, black politicians in DC fought for the right to rule themselves and not by the previously used setup of a board of commissioners. In 1973, the city was granted home rule by Congress and Walter Washington became the first official mayor of Washington, DC. Today, DC is still governed by a mayor and thirteen-person council, yet executive authority of the city still lies in the hands of Congress. DC's position as a federal city, subject to the rule of Congress, exacerbates and contributes to the tension between class and race that already exists and disenfranchises the urban poor. Amid this local urban landscape, black people in DC face similar problems as black communities nationwide, including the renewed interest in combating police brutality that has propelled the Black Lives Matter movement. The musical practices of the go-go community offer an affirmation of black humanity and resistance to oppression that speak to the struggles of black people not only in DC but also nationwide.

In order to understand go-go's contemporary connection to Black Lives Matter, it is important to consider the history of the genre. Go-go music was pioneered in the 1970s by bands such as Chuck Brown and the Soul Searchers, Trouble Funk, and Experience Unlimited. The title of the genre comes from keeping people going and going on the dance floor, because the beat, commonly known as "the pocket," continues between songs. Because of this continuous performance style where music can go on for an hour or more without a break, go-go music is best experienced in a live setting. Since the 1970s, go-go has been the sound of black DC, also known as the Chocolate City for its high demographic of black residents. Go-gos can be found in DC on almost every night of the week, and go-go musicians, through extended call and response, assert a philosophy that the audience is a part of the band. Although go-go music has roots in funk and Latin American rhythms, it ultimately serves as an example of West African retentions within African American musical practice (Maultsby 2000). At its core, go-go is a genre in which the concepts of music and dance are inseparable.

Although go-go music lies well within the conventions of the black musical aesthetic, it is a difficult genre to describe, because fans of the genre say that you don't know go-go until you have been to one.[6] In these environments, go-go music is almost more felt than heard, as an embodied sense of musical community. This is a broad, monolithic view of go-go music, when in fact the scene has several subgenres of its own. Some bands are old school, coming dressed in matching suits and having their choreography down pat. Some bands, branding themselves as "grown and sexy," are closer to contemporary R&B than funk music, playing cover songs over go-go beats. The youngest generation of go-go is called "bounce beat," and it was developed in 2003 by TCB (Total Control Band).[7] Bounce beat is more percussive than the funk-derived old school, thriving on a pulse rather than a swing beat.

Throughout its history, the major events and trends in the go-go community have both reflected and been shaped by key social issues within the black population of DC. This connection has historically revolved around the violence associated with the crack epidemic of the 1980s and 1990s. During this period, DC was known as the "murder capital," and the violence spilled into go-go shows, resulting in the music being banned at a number of clubs in DC and Maryland (Hopkinson 2012, 35). Although the violence in the city has waned, go-go is still stigmatized as a potentially violent activity, which keeps musicians from being able to book and retain venues. Natalie Hopkinson has documented this history, noting that "club owners of various races and ethnicities openly banned the music, keeping deejays from playing the rump-shaking music and turning away bands that carried the telltale conga-drum sets. DC politicians often railed against the music as a magnet for violence and illicit activity. A few politicians in Maryland and the District pursued aggressive campaigns to yank liquor licenses of venues hosting go-go music" (2012, 3) In the first two decades of the twenty-first century, in a rapidly gentrifying DC, go-go music is being displaced along with black residents. In fact, 2011 marked the first time in fifty years that DC's population has dropped to fewer than 50 percent African American, and go-go, as a result, has moved further into the suburbs of Maryland and Virginia (Morello and Keating 2011).

AFFIRMATION

My understanding of the affirmation of humanity is based on a discussion of blackness provided by the ethnomusicologist Mellonee Burnim in her work on the black gospel music tradition. She argues that, in affirming their blackness, "the African-American gained the power to reject the rites, beliefs, and values of the white society and particularly, the white church" (1985, 153). In the context of the Black Lives Matter movement, to say "Black Lives Matter" and to participate in the movement is to reject the values of a mainstream society that regularly dehumanizes black people. To reject dehumanization and to center and celebrate blackness in this way is to affirm black humanity.

In the context of the go-go community, this affirmation presents itself both inside of and outside of musical performances. Michelle Blackwell, a veteran go-go singer who currently performs with What Band 2.0, explained in an interview what it was like to play through the tragedies that had occurred over the summer. Blackwell compared the go-go to a church, saying that people were attending go-gos in order to heal. She also highlighted the intimacy of go-go venues, because they are playing for relatively small crowds of people in clubs rather than concert halls or stadiums. As a result of this high level of intimacy, she said that they were "up close and personal with their people," celebrating birthdays, anniversaries, and graduations year-round (Blackwell 2016). Go-go music's emphasis on the audience often extends to individual audience members. People can have specific events in their life shouted out during a go-go show so that they can be uplifted and celebrated by the entire audience. Performers are made aware of these events through a variety of methods; for example, audience members wearing T-shirts with names or neighborhoods on them or establishing a personal relationship with a band member (Chuck Brown used to have notes passed up to him from the audience to read off audience members' birthdays or other celebrations). In the context of performance, these events become rhythmically incorporated into the music that is already being performed. The announcement of a birthday does not stop the go-go: it becomes a part of the performance, and a necessary part at that. By emphasizing these celebrations, Blackwell situates the go-go as a space for black affirmation and survival, emphasizing her role in these practices of healing and celebration. No matter what happens during the week, black people can attend go-gos to replenish themselves.

In addition to affirmation within the performances themselves, go-go musicians also engage in a great deal of community work. For example, Experience Unlimited regularly performs at community days, which are events that celebrate a particular neighborhood in DC, specifically those that are majority black. High Quality Band recently performed at a youth correctional facility, which struck me as important and affirming because of the ways in which the prison industrial complex works to disenfranchise and disrupt the lives of black people, particularly black males. In *The New Jim Crow: Mass Incarceration in the Age of Colorblindness,* Michelle Alexander cites the disturbing statistic that in Washington, DC, three out of four black males "can expect to serve time in prison" (2012, 6). In keeping with the ideals of Black Lives Matter, the go-go community supports the idea that the most marginalized are in need of affirmation.

The local engagement of the go-go community extends from performances to pedagogy, with several pioneering go-go musicians teaching go-go history in DC public schools throughout the school year through a Teaching for Change initiative called "Teach the Beat." Working with a variety of age groups in classes throughout the city, these musicians teach children about their city's music, telling them the stories of how go-go came to be. John Buchanan, a pioneering go-go musician most famous for his work with Chuck Brown and the Soul Searchers, is one of the musicians that participates in "Teach the Beat." When describing his experiences as an educator, he noted, "There's a need there. The kids appreciated it, they respected it, what we were doing. It's nice, and I look forward to doing a lot more with them" (2016).

The community engagement work I have described above uplifts DC's overlooked black community, and in many cases, this internal work goes largely unnoticed. This work is conducted largely within black spaces, moving away from the white gaze. The white gaze refers to the ways in which the experiences of black people are often distorted through the racialized observances of white people (Yancy 2008). In the same vein, one of the central criticisms of Black Lives Matter is "why don't black activists care about black-on-black crime?" Scholars such as Natalie Hopkinson and David Wilson have debunked the focus on black-on-black crime as a narrative that ignores the structural violence inflicted on black communities. In describing the rise of the term in the 1980s, Wilson argues that "at the core of the violence, in renditions, was blackness rather than poverty, economics, or class. Instead of economic circumstance or social situatedness, race was the template applied to understand the violence" (2005, 4). Furthermore, Hopkinson argues that "there is a moral imperative to challenge these assumptions, that the term is slander against law abiding African-Americans, and that it refuses to acknowledge the effects of imposed segregation" (2010). The criticism that black activists ignore the crime within black neighborhoods and communities ignores the constant internal work and mobilizations that black people have been doing for years. I had the opportunity to interview Dominic Moulden, one such community organizer in DC. When asked about his work in the 1980s, he remarked that

> one of the things that frustrates people like me is that for all our lives, our churches, our community centers, our parents, uncles, aunts, and other relatives have been critiquing not only the violence that is within our communities but the social structures that create the violence in this capitalist system. So, one of the pressing issues at the time was that black churches that I worked for at the time, we were going around collecting guns from people. And I had to remind somebody about that, who had never heard me talk about that. There were so many things that we were doing that people ignored, because it was black people doing it, and then the colonized space wasn't being colonized at that point. (Moulden 2016)

Moulden highlights these core black institutions that have resisted violence, both inside and outside of the black community. He also inserts a critique of gentrification, noting that one of the reasons that people have become interested in community work is because they are being gentrified and therefore need to be "cleaned up." The kind of internal work that Moulden alludes to is often ignored in both Black Lives Matter and the go-go community, and I make this point to argue that black affirmation is crucial, whether it is visible to a broader, whiter audience or not. The same holds true for resilience as a characteristic of the movement.

Resilience

One of the core components of state oppression is surveillance. The go-go community's resilience (and resistance) to this tracking comes largely in the form of flexibility amid tracking and surveillance. From flexibility of performance venues, to naming and advertising, the go-go community is able to evade any total shutdown by staying on the move. Furthermore, because of the stigma of violence associated with the music, go-go band names are sometimes left off of flyers and shows are advertised through word of mouth. If word gets out that a go-go band is playing a show, high insurance costs can lead to the show being canceled.

The oppressive surveillance of black people, especially by the police, is a thread of continuity between Black Lives Matter and go-go. In her 2015 book *Dark Matters*, the sociologist Simone Browne argues that "surveillance in and of life is a fact of blackness" (6). Black bodies are tracked throughout society under the guise of a number of different justifications, often related to a perceived black criminality, which leads to violence enacted onto black bodies. Surveillance is both the event that sparked the formation of Black Lives Matter and also a prevalent issue in go-go music. Reiterating Alicia Garza, it was the murder of Trayvon Martin, a black body, a black *somebody* who was stalked before he was shot and killed by George Zimmerman, that led to the creation of Black Lives Matter.

Similarly, the Metropolitan Police Department has notoriously kept a go-go report that allowed them to track and shut down go-gos. This report, originally published by the *Washington City Paper* in 2010, includes the names of bands, addresses of venues, dates of performances, and, in many cases, starting and ending times (Smith 2010). It is also worth noting that many of the venues listed are in Maryland, not in Washington, DC, although it is not known how the Prince George's County (Maryland) Police Department participated in the gathering of these reports. The police department boasted at a news conference that this tracking was helping to lower the murder rate and move DC away from the "murder capital" nickname (Hopkinson 2012, 4).

This go-go report is situated within a long history of the surveillance of black bodies and black gathering spaces. In DC, this history resides in the Black Codes, laws passed in 1808 that detailed what was to be lawful and unlawful in the lives of black people, both free and enslaved (Price 1998). Those laws were extensive, ranging from the cruel ("When runaway slaves can be lawfully killed by their pursuers") to the absurd ("Punishment of slaves for flying kites"). Within these codes, two are of particular interest to the concept of assembly. The first, the Prohibition of Assemblages of Colored Persons, decreed that all assemblages of black people, except for religious meetings supervised by white men, were unlawful (Worthington 1848). The second is similar, outlawing private, secret, and religious meetings past 10 p.m. The second law went further in that it also implicated the police, saying that if a policeman did not shut the meetings down after gaining knowledge of them, he was liable to be fined. Therefore, we see how the police became a tool of the state, used specifically to track and suppress black people.

In addition to these local examples of resilience amid surveillance, go-go musicians also center themselves within the national struggle for black freedom through performance. Backyard Band, a band that has been one of the central pillars of the community for almost thirty years, recently performed in #blacklivesmatter t-shirts bearing the name of Sandra Bland, who died in police custody in the summer of 2015. In fact, the performance in which these shirts were worn was featured in a short documentary published by *The Atlantic* on how go-go musicians are navigating gentrification. Within this documentary, Backyard Band's lead mic, Anwan "Big G" Glover, commented on how go-go music is being affected by issues such as gentrification, saying that "it's changing because you have a lot of people moving here, that's really not go-go friendly. It's hard to really grasp it because the state of D.C. is not D.C. anymore. It's not chocolate city because you have so many people from everywhere. We still here, but a lot of people have migrated, a lot of people have left" (*The Atlantic* 2015). By performing in #sayhername shirts while working against processes of gentrification, Big G and the Backyard Band serve as an example of how go-go musicians are situated within both a national and a local struggle to protect both themselves and their music.

Playing covers of songs can also be a way to situate a go-go band within the context of Black Lives Matter. Covers have been a large part of go-go sets for decades, to the disappointment of many of the founding musicians, who think that a dependence on covers is what has kept go-go from receiving national attention. As mentioned above, SOS has covered Beyoncé's "Freedom," whose music video for the song features the mothers of Trayvon Martin, Mike Brown, and Eric Garner. Also, the Vybe Band regularly covers Kendrick Lamar's "Alright" during their Friday night sets. Even within a party, the power emanating from a crowd of black people chanting Lamar's hook, "We gon' be alright," is palpable and empowering.

It is within this aspect of performance that I locate the overlapping of affirmation and resilience most clearly. These two concepts do not exist in isolation but instead inform and support each other, especially within the context of go-go performance. To be resilient is to affirm black humanity, and to affirm black humanity is a radical act of self-care that is well within the realm of both resilience and resistance. Even as the go-go community faces erasure within a gentrifying Washington, DC, the go-go functions as a space of both healing and mourning, a place where black people can be human.

CONCLUSION

My goals for this chapter were twofold. First, with regard to stories about go-go music, I wanted to shift the narrative around go-go music from one of violence and criminality to one of activism. For decades, locals and institutions have held go-go responsible for a great deal of the violence in DC. Such narratives are the result of structural racism. The violence that exists in many black DC neighborhoods would exist with or without go-go, which is a genre that was and continues to be created in spite of and because of these circumstances. By framing go-go through an activist lens, I highlight the positive accomplishments of go-go musicians and go-go culture. I say this, knowing that go-go musicians themselves would not necessarily characterize themselves as activists, and that this imposition brings up questions of negotiating academic authority as well as what it means to be an activist within the black community.

Second, I intended to use this chapter to contribute to an unfinished conversation about politicized scholarship, and the politicization of ethnomusicology in particular. In January of 2017, as a response to the 2016 presidential election, the Society for Ethnomusicology released a brief statement, part of which is reprinted here:

> In the weeks following our conference it has become clear that our work is more important now than ever. The uncertain future of this new era, where powerful words and their aftershocks have put vulnerable groups at risk both symbolically and, in some cases, visibly, within our own communities, is a mandate for us to publicly reaffirm our long held values of inclusivity and tolerance; to disseminate our research, teaching, and activism in ways that are more public and more political; to share best practices; and to offer our voices and our commitment to the communities in which we live and work, local and global, wherever and whenever possible. (Society for Ethnomusicology 2017)

The politicization of my scholarship involves bringing to the fore the ways in which I have grappled with the everyday violence encountered in fieldwork, in the academy, and in black urban life. With this sentiment in mind, I return to the night of July 8th. I did not originally come to see the SOS band. They were opening for the Junkyard Band, one of the pioneering groups in go-go's history. However, while watching the videos of protesters on Twitter, I became overwhelmed with the idea that if I continued to watch, I would see someone being killed by the police on my phone. I then left the club before the Junkyard Band performed, determined that if I were going to bear witness to yet another black death I was going to do it alone, so that I could mourn alone. It is important to note that this fear was neither irrational nor isolated, as videos of black death have been circulated and recirculated constantly. As important as it is to bear witness, it is also particularly traumatizing to watch the death of an unarmed black person. I offer this story to provide just a small glimpse into the emotional labor involved in doing this work, and to contextualize my place in it. When I mark the go-go as a space for black people to be human, I am affirming my own humanity in the process.

Notes

1. Alton Sterling was unarmed, killed while selling CDs outside of a convenience store. Castile's death was live-streamed by his girlfriend, Diamond Reynolds. Pulled over for a broken tail light, Castile was shot while still in his vehicle, after informing the officer of his concealed carry permit (CNN 2016).

2. Pantaleo was not indicted for the murder of Eric Garner, despite the fact that the chokehold was ruled illegal by the New York Police Department in 1993.

3. The toxic water crisis of Flint, Michigan that began in 2014 has been attributed to environmental racism and to "the state government's blatant disregard for the lives and health of poor and black residents of a distressed city" (*New York Times* 2016).

4. A White House petition to designate Black Lives Matter as a "terror group" gained 141,000 signatures in July 2016 (Flores 2016).

5. Established in 1867, Howard University is one of the most prestigious HBCUs (Historically Black College and University) in the country.

6. Go-go is both an event and a genre; you go to the go-go to see a go-go band play go-go music.

7. Despite the similar name, bounce beat is of no relation to New Orleans "bounce" music, which is a subgenre of rap music with a much faster tempo than bounce beat. New Orleans bounce began in the early 1990s whereas the go-go bounce beat was not created until 2003. Furthermore, the stark differences in tempo lend themselves to different dance styles: "twerking" for New Orleans bounce, and "beat ya feet" for bounce beat, a dance form that originated in the black neighborhoods of the DMV (Washington DC, Maryland, and Virginia).

Works Cited

Alexander, Michelle. 2012. *The New Jim Crow: Mass Incarceration in the Age of Colorblindness*. New York: New Press.

Armah, Esther. 2012. "Emotional Justice." *The Network Journal*, March 18, 2012. https://tnj.com/emotional-justice/

Asch, Chris Myers, and George Derek Musgrove. 2016. "'We Are Headed for Some Bad Trouble': Gentrification and Displacement in Washington, D.C., 1910–2014." In *Capital Dilemma: Growth and Inequality in Washington, D.C.*, edited by Derek Hyra and Sabiyha Prince, 107–135. New York: Routledge.

The Atlantic. 2015. *Keeping Go-Go Going in a Gentrifying D.C.* Documentary, 5:42. https://www.theatlantic.com/video/index/417780/keeping-go-go-going-in-a -gentrifying-dc/

Blackwell, Michelle. 2016. Interview with Alison Martin, July 18, 2016. "A Right to the City." Exhibition Records, Anacostia Community Museum Archives. Washington, DC: Smithsonian Institution.

Bohlman, Philip V. 2008. "Other Ethnomusicologies, Another Musicology: The Serious Place of Disciplinary Alterity." In *The New (Ethno) Musicologies* edited by Henry Stobart, 95–114. Lanham, MD: Rowman and Littlefield.

Browne, Simone. 2015. *Dark Matters: On the Surveillance of Blackness.* Durham, NC: Duke University Press.

Buchanan, John. 2016. Interview with Alison Martin, June 21. "A Right to the City." Exhibition Records, Anacostia Community Museum Archives. Washington, DC: Smithsonian Institution.

Burnim, Mellonee. 1985. "The Black Gospel Music Tradition: A Complex of Ideology, Aesthetic, and Behavior." In *More Than Dancing: Essays on Afro-American Music and Musicians*, edited by Irene V. Jackson, 147–167. Westport, CT: Greenwood.

CNN. 2016. "Two Police Shootings, Two Videos, Two Black Men Dead," CNN, July 7, 2016. http://www.cnn.com/2016/07/07/us/shootings-alton-sterling-philando-castile/.

Flores, Reena. 2016. "White House Responds to Petition to Label Black Lives Matter a 'Terror' Group." *CBS News*, July 17, 2016.

Garza, Alicia. 2014. "A Herstory of the #BlackLivesMatter Movement." *The Feminist Wire*, October 7, 2014. Accessed March 2, 2017. http://www.thefeministwire.com /2014/10/blacklivesmatter-2/

Gillette Jr., Howard. 2011. *Between Justice and Beauty: Race, Planning, and the Failure of Urban Policy in Washington.* Baltimore, MD: Johns Hopkins University Press.

Hopkinson, Natalie. 2010. "The Myth of Black-on-Black Violence." *The Root*, June 16, 2010. https://www.theroot.com/the-myth-of-black-on-black-violence-1790879872

Hopkinson, Natalie. 2012. *Go-Go Live: The Musical Life and Death of a Chocolate City.* Durham, NC: Duke University Press.

Hunter, Marcus Anthony, Mary Pattillo, Zandria F. Robinson, and Keeanga-Yamahtta Taylor. 2016. "Black Placemaking: Celebration, Play, and Poetry." *Theory, Culture & Society* 33 (7–8): 31–56.

Kelley, Robin D. G. 2016. "What Does Black Lives Matter Want?" *Boston Review*, August 17, 2016.

Lowery, Wesley. 2015. "A Disproportionate Number of Black Victims in Fatal Traffic Stops." *Washington Post*, December 24, 2015.

Maultsby, Portia K. 2000. "Afrikanisms in African-American Music." In *A Turbulent Voyage: Readings in African American Studies*, edited by Floyd W. Hayes, 156–176. Lanham, MD: Rowman and Littlefield.

McQuirter, Marya Annette. 2003. "A Brief History of African Americans in Washington, D.C." *Cultural Tourism D.C.* https://www.culturaltourismdc.org/portal/a-brief-history-of-african-americans-in-washington-dc

Morello, Carol, and Dan Keating. 2011. "Number of Black D.C. Residents Plummets as Majority Status Slips Away." *Washington Post*, March 24, 2011.

Moulden, Dominic. 2016. Interview with Samir Meghelli and author, July 20. "A Right to the City" Exhibition Records, Anacostia Community Museum Archives. Washington, DC:

Smithsonian Institution.

New York Times. 2016. "The Racism at the Heart of Flint's Crisis." *New York Times.* March 25, 2016. https://www.nytimes.com/2016/03/25/opinion/the-racism-at-the-heart-of-flints-crisis.html

Price, Tanya Y. 1998. "White Public Spaces in Black Places: The Social Reconstruction of Whiteness in Washington, D.C." *Urban Anthropology and Studies of Cultural Systems and World Economic Development* 27 (3/4): 301–44.

Smith, Rend. 2010. "Once Again, MPD Helps You Party: The Latest Go-Go Report." *Washington City Paper,* July 27, 2010.

Society for Ethnomusicology. 2017. "Position Statement in Response to the 2016 U.S. Presidential Election." January 9, 2017. http://www.ethnomusicology.org/news/325267/Position-Statement-in-Response-to-the-2016-U.S.-Presidential-Election.htm

"A Vision for Black Lives." 2016. The Movement for Black Lives, August 1, 2016. policy.m4bl.org.

Washington Post. 2012. "Audio: Calls from Zimmerman, Neighbor Capture Last Minutes of Martin's Life." *Washington Post.* May 20, 2012. http://www.washingtonpost.com/wp-srv/special/nation/last-minutes-trayvon-martin-911-calls/-

Wilson, David. 2005. *Inventing Black-on-Black Violence: Discourse, Space, and Representation.* Syracuse, NY: Syracuse University Press.

Worthington, Garrettson Snethen. 1848. *The Black Code of the District of Columbia, in Force September 1st, 1848.* New York: A. & F. Anti-Slavery Society.

Yancy, George. 2008. *Black Bodies, White Gazes: The Continuing Significance of Race.* Lanham, MD: Rowman and Littlefield.

ALISON MARTIN is a PhD candidate in the Department of Folklore and Ethnomusicology at Indiana University. Her dissertation work focuses on the intersections of gentrification, race, and sound in Washington, DC.

FIVE

BLACK DETROIT: SONIC DISTORTION FUELS SOCIAL DISTORTION

Denise Dalphond

DETROIT BOASTS ENTREPRENEURIAL, INDEPENDENT APPROACHES to creativity and the music industry, and it celebrates African American culture as Black cultural nationalism. Detroit's Black dance music spaces are renegade spaces that provide the platform for Black liberation.[1] This spirit of independence has played an important role in the Black musical communities of Detroit, beginning with the blues and jazz scenes of the 1940s, followed by the establishment of the Motown Record Corporation. This legacy formed the foundation of electronic music and dance music culture. Detroit's Black cultural nationalism provides affirming spaces for diverse communities to celebrate African American culture in a city with a Black population that has surpassed 80 percent for much of the twentieth century and into the twenty-first (US Census Bureau 2016). Techno and house music in Detroit contribute revolutionary cultural offerings to the Black Lives Matter movement with a powerful collection of musical projects that testify to the varied stories of Black liberation.

The musical recordings and cultural philosophy of Underground Resistance (UR), Moodymann, and Drexciya offer rich cultural soundscapes on which to base this study of Black liberation and the emergence of the Black Lives Matter movement in the city of Detroit. Protest also occurs on the ground in Detroit at Black dance parties that are often policed aggressively by law enforcement; for example, Theo Parrish hosts and DJs events that serve a dual purpose as Black dance parties and protest in performance. On Friday, May 26, 2017, the Detroit police department invaded and shut down one of the most prominent events in the city during Movement Festival weekend, which is a historically important annual three-day event in Detroit techno and house music.[2] These artists offer powerful, revolutionary art in a way that is unapologetically Black and radical, a message that has become a powerful tenet of the Black Lives Matter movement.[3] Detroit contributes renegade musical culture to Black Lives Matter's consciousness-raising activism in a world steeped in white supremacy and anti-Black hatred and violence. Black Lives Matter's guiding principles are founded on "restorative justice," and its founders state, "We are unapologetically Black in our positioning. In affirming that Black Lives Matter, we need not qualify our position. To love and desire freedom and justice for ourselves is a necessary prerequisite for wanting the same for others" (Black Lives Matter 2017). Black cultural nationalism in Detroit paired with radical social ideologies and entrepreneurial musical commerce answers this demand for restorative justice. Representation, self-protection via artistic and economic independence, and mythological cultural nationalism mark Detroit as a site ripe for these fertile beginnings of the Black Lives Matter movement.

African American DJs and producers create and perform in a variety of musical worlds, ranging from the insular life of Detroit to the international realm of DJ culture, which has amassed a global fan base and sonic soundscape formulated partly by the appropriation and fusion of Black music in the United States and Europe. Electronic music in Detroit emerged among African Americans during the 1970s and 1980s before the genre was actually called techno. Early producers and DJs of this music were mostly young middle-class Black women and men who listened to remarkably eclectic local radio, and were surrounded by a burnt, crumbling, sometimes dangerous urban landscape plagued by poverty, corrupt political leadership, drug-related crime, and a habitually contentious relationship with the police. Charles "Electrifying Mojo" Johnson and Jeff Mills as the Wizard are significant figures in Detroit radio of the late 1970s, 1980s, and early 1990s. Mojo impacted listeners with his eclectic multigenre approach to musical selection and sharing. He presented a vast range of musical styles to his listeners, playing anything from electro-funk, disco, pop, hip hop, German electronic rock, classical music, rhythm & blues, and rock. Mills played many genres, but listeners primarily heard hip hop and electronic music mixed at a remarkably fast pace. The Wizard impacted listeners with his technically precise and impossibly fast mixing style (Todd Osborn, interview with author, September 12, 2008). Like other iconic Black radio personalities in other cities, Electrifying Mojo and the Wizard served as critical and significant voices, providing social commentary, musical education, and entertainment on air.

Producers began making music in the 1980s, reacting to the urban environments in which they lived. Inspired by the relative overabundance of desolation, these artists created music, stories, and visual art about utopian contexts and activities that they likened to space travel, underwater dwelling, futuristic technology, or, simply, a better version of Black life in Detroit. The first two Detroit techno releases came in 1981 by A Number of Names and Cybotron.[4] Their music was not yet called "techno," but their style signaled a new genre of music that was distinctly from Detroit. Techno's musical characteristics include percussive rhythms typically in common meter (4/4), with tempos ranging from 120 to 150 bpm. There is an emphasis on polyrhythm, infusing a funkiness that is a distinctive quality of Detroit techno and house, and Black electronic music. Complex layering of rhythmic patterns and emphasis on the back beat (the second and fourth beats of each measure) is typical of techno music produced by Detroit artists, and is less commonly performed by European and white American techno producers.

Detroit DJs and producers, both Black and white, navigate the cultural complexities linking the familiar, largely African American sonic culture in Detroit with extensive networks of transglobal remakes, reinterpretations, and original sounds. European appropriation and reinterpretation helped bring electronic music to white audiences in the United States in the 1980s; however, Detroit's electronic music culture has consistently boasted a diverse community, both in ethnic (African American, Latinx, Asian American, and white) and sexual identity (straight, LGBTQ, and gender nonconforming) since its inception.[5] Faced with real co-option of cultural and social identity through appropriation, many African Americans in Detroit protect cultural heritage by reclaiming ownership and power over musical creativity, production, and circulation, thereby keeping their art local. That is, all elements of the contemporary music industry operate in Detroit: composition, recording and production, mastering, vinyl pressing, distribution, sales, both in record shops and online, and dance parties. During a round-table discussion at the Roots of Techno Conference at Indiana University in 2006, Theo Parrish and Minx (a Detroit producer and DJ) explain Black entrepreneurship in Detroit, comparing the sound quality of two different records.[6]

> THEO: The levels are identical. I'll illustrate two things: what was going on in Chicago in 1987 and what was going on in Detroit in 1987—and difference in pressings. [Theo plays "Move It."] . . . I was in Chicago at the time. One thing I always appreciated about Detroit records is you could hear the highs in those records, . . . the crispest highs.

To illustrate his point, he played two tracks from 1987 on the turntables: "Move It" by Rhythim Is Rhythim (Derrick May), produced in Detroit, and "Frequency" by Lil' Louis, produced in Chicago.

> MINX: The pressing is totally different, two different pressing plants.
>
> THEO: Exactly. Those are the different pieces of quality control that became specific to Detroit and to Chicago. . . . In Chicago, . . . there weren't really a lot of Black artists owning the labels, whereas in Detroit, we owned our labels, and we still do. We might have had a little bit of a shoddy pressing, but we still owned our masters.

The audience heard it clearly: Black musicians in Detroit own Black music in Detroit, thus demarcating a Detroit-centered sonic revolution.

DETROIT'S SONIC REVOLUTION

Institutionalized white supremacy, and rebellion that threatened white supremacy, brought destruction to much of Detroit's landscape throughout the middle portion of the twentieth century, culminating in the 1967 race rebellion. This local migration paired with the local automobile industry marked Oakland County, bordering the city of Detroit along Eight Mile Road, among the wealthiest in the country for many years (Wolffe 2010). Jerry Heron, Professor of English at Detroit's Wayne State University, and a Detroit techno pioneer, Jeff Mills, testify to these trends in Detroit's history:

> What happened in 1967 specifically in Detroit is that a long pattern of exclusionary practices, a long pattern of segregation, both legal and quasi-legal in the city simply erupted into violence. . . . Then it became convenient to say "That's why we did what we did," instead of investigating the actual reasons

why we did what we did. That is, we decided to depopulate cities at the end of World War II, we didn't decide to depopulate cities the day after the so-called riot in 1967. (Heron, in Bredow 2006)

Imagine a city that was designed for four million people, that less than a million people only occupy now. (Mills, in Bredow 2006)

Severe economic challenges, deepened by the infiltration of drugs and violent gang culture in the 1980s, and a persistent lack of leadership from corrupt municipal officials, led to a disheartening decline in city life. The emptiness offered by population exodus allowed those who remained, whether by choice or necessity, to get creative.

Detroit's citizens live with minimal official oversight due to corruption at all levels of municipal government, which offers some creative freedom, but also signifies widespread poverty and severe lack of basic city services like safe public education, police and fire protection, and snow and trash removal.[7] For some, isolation leads to incubation. In an interview with Mark Fisher for *The Wire* magazine, the musician and recording company owner Mike Banks explained this isolation in detail, as well as his active response to it as a musician,

Detroit was going to be the model city for people to own cars with, and it is: our freeway system is so extensive, you can get from the suburbs fifty miles out, it take you twenty minutes to get downtown, but it take my mother, who lives in the city, an hour and a half on the bus to get downtown . . . because right now, if you don't own a car and have insurance, or you can't afford the gas, then you can't move. So we got a landlocked city[,] man, and it's deteriorating. (Banks, quoted in Fisher 2007)

This isolation affects people's identities as musicians in significant ways. Some internalize the isolation as desolation and negativity in other forms, and this informs their musical creativity. However, isolation suits introverted personalities well, as explained by the DJ and producer Brendan Gillen: "Techno, individual music, allows people that have more difficulties in society relating to people, to make music, and make excellent music by themselves, and do the one awesome thing that they can do. The awesome thing that they can do is not hanging out, not being a community leader: it's making these music statements" (Brendan M. Gillen, interview with author, July 22, 2009).

Electronic music, which is primarily instrumental, offers an outlet when words are inadequate or uninspiring. The expressive mobilizing power in Detroit house and techno is made evident in the rhythmic and melodic patterns as well as in the ideologies and stories. The ethnomusicologist Noriko Manabe examines twenty-first-century protest music and street democracy in Japan, and explores the force of music in mobilizing political resistance. Manabe explores space, public and private, tangible and intangible, and the ways in which people, including musicians, mobilize and educate themselves toward action. "In post-3.11 Japan, public protests have played a major part in raising awareness of the problems with nuclear power and building solidarity among anti-nuclear citizens. Music is integral to these protests" (Manabe 2015, 176).[8] Similarly in Detroit, music provides a mobilizing outlet but often without vocables. Detroit techno and house music challenge white supremacy while simultaneously destroying the boundaries of what is typically and traditionally understood as Black musical culture. Underground Resistance, Drexciya, Moodymann, and Theo Parrish built their ideologies of resistance in the underground and they formulated them in such a way that they have remained underground and safeguarded; a protective stance that helps maintain unapologetic Black ownership of Black musical culture. Underground culture can be defined geographically, socially, culturally, and sonically. The ethnomusicologist Kai Fikentscher uses the concept "underground" in his work on dance music: "The prefix 'underground' does not merely serve to explain that the associated type of music—and its cultural context—are familiar only to a small number of informed persons. Underground also points to the sociopolitical function of the music, framing it as one type of music that in order to have meaning and continuity is kept away . . . from mainstream society, mass media, and those empowered to enforce prevalent moral and aesthetic codes and values" (2000, 5). This formulation of underground pairs well with Noriko Manabe's explorations of music as resistance. Sonic distortion is revolutionary because underground cultural infrastructure protects the sound in the city, and at the same time, "the cityscape changes with the sound" (Manabe 2015, 261).

The underground as a cultural concept holds significant weight and cultural meaning in Detroit and around the world in electronic dance music culture. From physical space to sound and visual aesthetics, the underground is formed through discourse. It is created through word of mouth, flyers, and other forms of communication about events and performance. Detroit's underground DJ and dance music culture often protects electronic music from appropriation and policing, but is not always successful. The club provides a vibrant local space for protest because it is typically the context for joy and celebration through gathering, listening, dancing, and partying. Parties in the 1970s were held in clubs and bars: the most noteworthy were Black gay dance clubs like Heaven and Todd's with crowds that were diverse in terms of sexual identity, race, ethnicity, class, and educational background. The underground was a safe haven to groups and individuals who suffered persecution and oppression in other social realms. Thus, Detroit culture nurtures ideologies of Black nationalism by providing avenues and spaces that are much safer for expression of Black identity than spaces that are typically dominated by white people and, structured or unstructured, white supremacist culture. Self-sufficiency and adaptation to global environmental changes, such as rising temperatures, rising sea levels, and quickly changing ecosystems, are fruitful forces here because of this isolation; African American culture has a space to flourish uninterrupted in a majority Black city.

BLACK LIVES MATTER: PROTEST IN PERFORMANCE AND MUSICAL MYTHOLOGY

On Friday, May 26, 2017, Theo Parrish hosted the sixth annual Music Gallery Detroit event.[9] The dance party was held at a community art center with a performance space in northeast Detroit called Talking Dolls. Information on the party flier referred to the event as an "intimate gathering" with "nourishment" provided by a local vegan Black woman chef. No cameras were allowed on the dance floor and Detroit residents got a generous 50 percent discount. This was an underground Black dance party in Detroit because it prioritized local guests, featured Black dance music, and the dance floor was safe for dancing, mild drug use (like joints and pills), and some consensual sexual activity. The party was scheduled from 11 p.m. to 7 a.m. The police arrived shortly after 2 a.m. and shut down the party. The following was written by Theo Parrish on his Sound Signature website and Facebook page on June 2, 2017, a few days following the party:

> We provide a serious sound system, keep the DJ from view, and let the music do the rest. We understand the power of release that music offers us, and feel

the need to spread that to our people, especially our community here in Detroit. . . . Folks come to town to make their money off of Black-made music in
a Black-made city. That's why during this time, it is especially important for
us to create our environment on our terms. . . . Joy is policed, especially when
it is to be had by people of color. . . . Hosts and attendees of color were threatened with violence and incarceration. Officers openly told attendees that they
"wanted to scare" people who they put into police cars and threatened with
arrest, for infractions that were punishable by fines at best. It is also notable
that most parties being held around the city were either visited by police without consequence, or weren't policed at all. We don't find it coincidental that
the parties allowed to continue were either festival-affiliated and/or hosted
by non-Black people. In a city that capitalizes on the abundant history and
presence of Black creativity, it is unsettling how easily the city can cast aside
those who have built its legacy to begin with. But with this we keep pushing
on. When music and dancing are policed we know that it is indeed powerful.
(Sound Signature 2017)

Drawing on Theo's words, I contend that Detroit can fuel widespread
white supremacy, dismantling revolution because the city provides the cultural inspiration for a world based on Black liberation.

Many local house and techno producers are renegades in their approach
to musical production and DJ culture, as well as in their cultural philosophies. Theo Parrish, Underground Resistance, Drexciya, and Moodymann
are among a few who offer powerful, creative approaches to global political
change through musical community building. Underground Resistance is a
Detroit techno group founded by Robert Hood, Jeff Mills (the Wizard), and
"Mad" Mike Banks. Banks also heads a distribution company, record label,
and production house in Detroit called Submerge, founded with Christa
Weatherspoon in 1992. Originally formulated as "Submerge Underground
Railroad: Detroit's First Mail-Order Musik Outlet," Underground Resistance invited consumers to "come and take a ride on Submerge's Underground Railroad, where the musical varieties will commute you through a
musical time vortex to the past, present and the next millennium."[10] Banks
mentors musicians, assisting them in launching record labels, mastering
and pressing music onto vinyl, which he then distributes through his well-
established, successful, and reliable global network.

Submerge is an essential institution in Detroit's electronic musical culture and to the international presence of this music. While electronic music
culture is celebrated as a communal activity, Detroit presents a soundscape

with equal opportunity for isolated musical creativity, innovation, and experimentation. Electronic music in Detroit, as a highly individual art form that involves intensive detailed work with multiple electronic machines, lends itself to intellectual experimentation. Musicians and musical institutions in Detroit embody this independent experimental ideology, establishing their music careers or businesses within an insulated, protective foundation while offering their fans large catalogs of music and vibrant performances, both in Detroit and around the world. For them, Detroit is a musically self-sufficient hub. Underground Resistance, Submerge, and the Somewhere in Detroit record store (located in Submerge's basement) represent the independence and global impact of this uniquely commercial music.

Submerge is located on East Grand Boulevard, one mile east of 2468 West Grand Boulevard, the location of Motown's first headquarters in Detroit, and a few blocks north of Planet E, the recording studio of the producer and recording company owner Carl Craig.[11] It is housed in a three-story orange-brick United Automobile Workers union building. Banks renovated and restored the building in the early 2000s. The space is nondescript on the outside. Without knowing the existing business inside, passersby only see an old brick building in a block of other old brick buildings. There are no Submerge signs indicating what is beyond the brick walls, no signs announcing it as the headquarters of Underground Resistance. There are no outside markers for the record shop in the basement, the Detroit techno museum on the ground floor, or the recording studios on the upper floors.

The front door of Submerge is always locked and under camera surveillance. To protect recording and production equipment from theft, business owners often avoid moving in through the front door and do not advertise on the street. Visitors must know of Submerge first to seek out its location. Appointments are typically required for entry. Once inside the Submerge building, however, visitors find that the tightly guarded exterior gives way to generous hospitality. Mike Banks exudes a stern, serious, tough demeanor. Like his building, his stern exterior quickly transforms into warmth, generosity, and exuberance. An outsider visiting Submerge for the first time, meeting caution at the front door, and then entering the rich cultural microcosm within will find this to be a worthy metaphor for Detroit artists protecting local innovative musical culture from appropriation. Outsiders stay out until invited in.

Submerge set the foundation for Black-owned independent musical creativity in Detroit, shaping local dance music culture into the self-sufficient electronic music hub that it is. I contextualize this history, marking the development of Submerge and Underground Resistance as the start of Detroit techno's institutionalization as a renegade art, but techno's intellectual history reaches further back to the music and ideas of Juan Atkins, Derrick May, Kevin Saunderson, and Eddie Fowlkes—Detroit techno's first producers. These four African American men based their creative philosophies on time travel and utopian living. The term *techno* and many other intellectual concepts that these early producers had in mind originated from the futurist Alvin Toffler's books *Future Shock* and *The Third Wave*. In these works, Toffler constructs a concept of "techno rebels," which the author Dan Sicko applies to producers and consumers of techno in Detroit. According to Sicko, this concept encompasses "people who are cautious of new, powerful technologies and want to temper the breakneck pace of technological advancement.... Techno's underlying philosophy has less to do with futurism, as is commonly believed, than with the power of the individual and personal visions of Utopia" (2010, 12). Shortly after Underground Resistance was established, Kenny Dixon Jr. (Moodymann, KDJ) began to record house and techno music. His musical catalogue is an example of a new, powerful vision of utopian existence, as explained by Sicko. Since his first release in 1994, his entire musical career has featured commentary on race and racism. His first LP in 1997 came with these liner notes, printed here as they appear on the album:

> i want to say "what's happenin'" to all the niggaz that live and die in detroit everyday. to all the unknown artists, producers and djs from around the globe, believe it or not, you're the ones keeping it live and real, all of the older brothers and sisters that are musicians that have never really made a dime but have more talent than most of the people in the business. and to all you white suburban kids, sampling black music all the time, try some rock 'n roll for a change, you're making black music sound silly, weak and tired and most of all a stranger. thanks to everyone from japan and europe and back to the states, you know who you are, if i was to start writing names, i would be writing continuously, for weeks. when you support KDJ, not only are you supporting me and my

whole entire family, but all the real niggaz from detroit who struggle everyday, just to live, eat and breathe.[12]

Kenny Dixon Jr. carries this insulated identity into his house and techno productions. He has spent his entire musical career communicating radical messages of antiracism. On a Moodymann release titled "J.A.N." in 2001 (J.A.N. stands for Just Another N***ah), KDJ uses samples of the legendary Detroit radio disc jockey Electrifying Mojo interviewing Prince, but Prince's voice does not appear in the song. Midway through the piece, listeners hear Mojo's voice asking, "What was it like growing up from Detroit?" Moodymann's message is in the music that follows the question. The melodic patterns sounding like a Fender Rhodes keyboard, a simple, repetitive bass line, and rhythmic snare patterns offer responses to Mojo's questions.

Moodymann released an LP in 2008 titled *Det.riot '67*, referencing race rebellions in Detroit during the summer of 1967. The fifth song on the LP, titled "Det.riot," includes the voice of what appears to be a white male newscaster reporting the events that led to the rebellion. The voice presents a picture of Detroit on July 23, 1967, stating that it was hot and bright, and thousands of sports fans were watching the Detroit Tigers play baseball. "It's doubtful any remember the day at the ballpark. July 23rd was the day the riots started." The music that follows is eerie, distorted, and funky. The voice continues to narrate about the "minor incident" and "routine police action." Kenny Dixon Jr. embodies local ideologies of independence and Black business ownership as the cornerstone of his musical activities. He displays a vibrant love for Detroit and Black culture in his music, his DJ sets, and his engagement of independent music commerce. In 2016, KDJ's most recent contribution to Detroit and Black cultural nationalism was the transformation of a large three-story home across East Grand Boulevard from Submerge into a brick-and-mortar dedication to Prince. All the windows have purple drapes and billow toward the street in warm weather. Inside are significant cultural artifacts documenting Prince's career. It is a work of art, whether you enter the building or appreciate it from the street. Moodymann also mentors younger producers, both women and men, in intentional ways, teaching them to work independently and to build self-sufficient musical careers. While not directly linked to UR, Moodymann is as much an institution as Submerge and UR because of his regular service to his city and his inspiring creativity.

Socially conscious approaches to music-making and music industry–building make Detroit a site ripe for the unapologetically Black ideological and political affirmations of the Black Lives Matter movement. Cultural, political, and social work toward Black liberation is a commitment "to collectively, lovingly, and courageously working . . . for freedom and justice for Black people, and by extension, all people," and techno provides a forum in which musicians can create and perform as social activists (Black Lives Matter 2017). Drexciya, a group created by Gerald Donald and James Stinson, formed a powerful narrative of resistance and ultimate sovereignty for people of color through the sonic, visual, and intellectual dimensions of their musical production and performance, releasing much of their music on the Submerge and Underground Resistance record labels. In the late 1980s, Donald and Stinson developed the Drexciyan sea narrative, which begins as an emancipation journey out of slavery and transitions into a powerful story similar to Plato's Atlantis, built out of Black liberation, and, ultimately, nationalism. The story goes as follows: Black women and men formed an underwater society after being discarded violently by colonialist human traffickers over the sides of ships. Some of the women were pregnant. While still in the womb, Drexciyan fetuses adapted to their deep-sea dwelling before birth and learned to survive underwater. Some Drexciyan citizens became researchers and scientists; they built a society based on intellectual sovereignty and physical strength that would thrive without white supremacy and, more importantly, without white people. A selection from the liner notes of *The Quest*, an LP released in 1997, describes the Drexciyan plan and origin story:

> Could it be possible for humans to breath [sic] underwater? A foetus [sic] in its mothers [sic] womb is certainly alive in an aquatic environment.

> During the greatest holocaust the world has ever known, pregnant America-bound African slaves were thrown overboard by the thousands during labour for being sick and disruptive cargo. Is it possible that they could have given birth at sea to babies that never needed air?

> Recent experiments have shown mice able to breathe liquid oxygen. Even more shocking and conclusive was a recent instance of a premature infant saved from certain death by breathing liquid oxygen through its undeveloped lungs. These facts combined with reported sightings of Gillmen and swamp monsters in the coastal swamps of the South-Eastern United States make the slave trade theory startlingly feasible.

Are Drexciyans water breathing, aquatically mutated descendants of those unfortunate victims of human greed? have they been spared by God to teach us or terrorize us? Did they migrate from the Gulf of Mexico to the Mississippi river basin and on to the great lakes of Michigan?

Do they walk among us? Are they more advanced than us and why do they make their strange music?

What is their Quest?
These are many of the questions that you don't know and never will.
The end of one thing . . . and the beginning of another.

Out—The Unknown Writer

Drexciyans built a society based on Black liberation. White human traffickers discarded Black women and men, thinking they were taking life from the people they tried to imprison in a global, institutionalized system of slave labor. In this emancipation narrative, African people, who had once been shackled, outsmarted white supremacists by defining their own freedom. White people continued to be land dwellers, oblivious to the formation of a massive underwater society that privileged intellect, strength, health, and commitment to evolution all at once. "Drexciya is the name of an underwater country populated by the unborn children of African women thrown off of middle passage slave ships that learned to breathe underwater in the womb" (Drexciya 1997, liner notes). "The Middle Passage" appears regularly in Drexciyan mythology. Once Drexciyans free themselves from the ship and landbound white captors, the direction of the story flips from human trafficking and enslaved labor toward independence and self-sustenance. Jumping ship replaces the usual narrative of the Middle Passage in this mythology. Drexciyans force the story below the earth's surface into underwater sea dwelling and liberation for people of color. They alter the course of racism, destroying it by creating a world without white supremacy: a Black nationalist world. The Drexciyan mission was ultimate inheritance of the earth without bringing harm to its citizens.

Kodwo Eshun states, in a study focused on Afrofuturism, "Drexciya have constructed a Black-Atlantean mythology that successfully speculates on the evolutionary code of black subjectivity" (2003, 300). To consider the reality of this Drexciyan world, fans of Drexciya and other revolutionaries need only to shift our minds beyond a world plagued by white supremacy.

Climate change demonstrates that Drexciyan citizens do not even have to enter into battle to demand reparations in this mythology. The earth already plans to take care of them with melting ice caps and swelling seas. The underwater narrative also suits Detroit Black underground culture, offering rich musical inspiration available through techno's underground network of global musical communication and consumption.

Drexciyans prioritize their music to tell their history. Sound is an essential element of Drexciyan social and cultural life. Music informs scientific developments, earthbound underwater travel, outer-space travel, intellectual advancements, and general cultural and social existence. Drexciyan citizens are Black people, and their music is Black music. The Drexciyan world echoes science-fiction, global-warming survival narratives: it exists before the earth's north and south poles melt, but Drexciyans created the possibility that when earth's surface is mostly covered in melted ice, people of color will be ready for survival and safe from destruction. This emancipation narrative is a metaphor for Black Detroit and the global project of ending racism and imperialism. Drexciya presents a story of strength, power, autonomy, and safety for people of color. Art can and must be at the forefront of any activism because of its potential to inspire and communicate world-changing ideas; as Toni Morrison states, "In times of dread, artists must never choose to remain silent" (2015, 184). This call resonates with Detroit's artists, and certainly with the work of Donald and Stinson. Their Drexciyan narrative of freedom encourages Black people to escape into a better past and envision a more hopeful present, while challenging white people to imagine a world without them. Life for people of color around the globe has been subject to racially based terror and violence much different from that of white people, who always benefit from white supremacy, and, therefore, that necessitates a radical reconceptualization to reconcile Black life with freedom and liberation. Detroit offers renegade art to the world to help fuel global consciousness-changing work. Drexciya challenges white listeners to release the captivating white supremacist ideologies and embrace the idea of a world in which white people are not supreme.

The Drexciyan catalog of EPs and LPs reads as a revelation of their philosophies.[13] Their first release in 1992 on Shockwave Records, a sublabel of the Underground Resistance record label, was titled *Deep Sea Dweller*. Drexciya and Underground Resistance ensured that the words printed on their mostly instrumental music releases communicated plans for rebellion with expert precision. The song titles on *Deep Sea Dweller* are as follows: "Sea Quake," "Nautilus 12," "Depressurization," and "Sea Snake." All four tracks are hard, fast Detroit techno, made up of driving pulses and complex melodic lines that flow at high speed. "Sea Quake" sounds like the initial rumblings of the Drexciyan society's beginnings. "Nautilus 12" introduces listeners to the sounds of the society in operation and its underwater ships. "Depressurization" sounds exactly like its title implies; the intro begins with melodic patterns instead of the hard and fast rhythms at the start of the two tracks on side A. The track allows the listener to understand what adapting to underwater life might sound like. Even the BMI publishing data involve protest: SW1007 Dance Threat Music. Finally, the fourth track on this legendary first release, titled "Sea Snake," challenges the most serious ethnomusicologist or music lover to sit still and focus. The melody begins first in the bass sounds of the intro. Donald and Stinson then introduce other sonic patterns at staggered intervals until all the layers of organized sound pour out of the speakers. "Sea Snake" is an inspiring piece of music that sounds at once like an underwater Black dance party, and the movements of a deep-sea-dwelling serpent that protects the boundaries of Drexciya while being a threat to white supremacist land dwellers, should they dare attempt to infiltrate.

Other LP, EP, and track titles by Drexciya include *Aquatic Invasion, Molecular Enhancement, Digital Tsunami, Neptune's Lair*, "Wavejumper," and "Bubble Metropolis."[14] The printed communication on *Bubble Metropolis* is powerful. Side A of the 12-inch vinyl record is titled "Fresh Water"; Side B, "Salt Water." Detroit techno releases on vinyl are not always given side A and side B names, but on this Drexciyan artifact, they are. Track titles on "Fresh Water" are "Aqua Worm Hole," "Positron Island," and "Beyond the Abyss." "Salt Water" track titles are "Bubble Metropolis," "Danger Bay," and conclude with "Welcome to DREXCIYA." These six tracks are a sonic document of the journey to Drexciya. It is not a safe, easy journey, and white people are not allowed entry. Side A also tells the listener, "Tracks made in Drexciya for UR in Detroit." Underground Resistance, the group and the record label, are often referred to as UR, and a phrase that often accompanies most printed material about UR is "For Those Who Know." Fans, listeners, dancers, and consumers are expected to do the work of educating ourselves to be worthy of entering Submerge or having access to UR's sonic documents. This phrase does not appear on *Bubble Metropolis*, but the idea is present. "Salt Water," side B, displays the words "Filtered by DREXCIYA," "Special Thanks to GOD," and "MAD MIKE & HYPERSPACE Publishing," because publishing rights ownership is an essential act of resistance and protest via entrepreneurship in a world bent on appropriating African American music and culture.

The liner notes in another release, *Aquatic Invasion*, set forth the connections between Drexciya and Underground Resistance in their communication to defend Drexciya's borders:

> On February First Nineteen Hundred And Ninety Five the Drexciyan Tactical Seaforces received orders from UR Strikeforce Command, for one final mission. The dreaded Drexciya stingray and barracuda battalions were dispatched from the Bermuda Triangle. Their search and destroy mission to be carried out during the Winter Equinox of 1995 against the programmer strongholds. During their return journey home to the invisible city one final mighty blow will be dealt to the programmers. Aquatic knowledge for those who know.
>
> The Unknown Writer

Subsequent releases connect underwater earth dwelling with other stellar bodies and systems beyond the solar system, and this part of the story is developed further, connecting ideas with early Detroit techno philosophies of utopian existence and space travel. On *Grava 4*, released in 2002, song titles include "Hightech Nomads," "Cascading Celestial Giants," and "Astronomical Guidepost," presenting this utopian, space-based ideology to listeners.[15] The Drexciyan project had further plans for travel and development, but James Stinson passed away in 2002. Kodwo Eshun explains of the *Grava 4* album, "For their *Grava 4* CD, released in 2002, the group contacted the International Star Registry in Switzerland to purchase the rights to name a star. Having named and registered their star 'Grava 4,' a new installment within their ongoing sonic fiction is produced. In wrapping their speculative fiction around electronic compositions that then locate themselves around an existing extraterrestrial space, Drexciya grant themselves the imperial right to nominate and colonize interstellar space" (2003, 301). Or perhaps, as we approach the year 2020, Drexciya might be a decolonizing force, as they represent freedom more than a new hierarchy.

Eshun, author of multiple texts on Afrofuturism, some based on unre-
corded ethnographic interviews with Drexiya co-founder Gerald Donald,[16]
confirms the desire for a utopian present over an imagined future. Eshun
presents ethnographic proof that Drexciya was interested in the utopian
present and all its space-travel possibilities, as opposed to waiting for the
future to catch up, and Dan Sicko confirms this perspective by stating,
"Techno's underlying philosophy has less to do with futurism, as is commonly believed, than with the power of the individual and personal visions
of Utopia" (2010, 12). Restorative justice concerns itself less with waiting for
the future, and more with changing the present. Afrofuturism's prioritizing
the future becomes an intellectual and analytical warning to readers and
thinkers because it is founded in a social context of waiting for the future to
arrive, something the future will never do. Further, and more onerous than
time, Afrofuturism essentializes Blackness into a monolithic identity that
lends itself frequently in scholarship to post-soul aesthetics; in order to be
of the future, African American culture must somehow exist beyond soul
(David 2017).

Local Detroit-centered approaches to cultural production, analysis, and
change guided my research and formulated my findings. Afrofuturism was
not an ethnographic topic of conversation. I did not raise the term or the
subject, but neither did anyone else; in a majority Black city like Detroit,
local social ideologies are present and are distinct from Afrofuturism. The
term and concept of Afrofuturism was first introduced by cultural critic
Mark Dery in 1993. He defines Afrofuturism as "Speculative fiction . . . and
more generally, African-American signification that appropriates images of
technology and a prosthetically enhanced future" (1993, 180). Dery, who is
white, casually goes on to explain: "In the context of what I've chosen to call
"Afrofuturism," that the mojos and goofer dust of Delta blues, together with
the lucky charms, fetishes, effigies, and other devices employed in syncretic
belief systems, such as voodoo, hoodoo, santeria, mambo, and macumba,
function very much like the joysticks, Datagloves, Waldos, and Spaceballs
used to control virtual realities" (210).

Dery's swift comfort with what he thinks is a list of African Diasporic and
African American cultural characteristics is disturbing, as is his ability to
link his list that contains the terms *goofer* and *lucky charms* to American cultural references like Spaceballs and greater financial access to video game

culture. Dery's Afrofuturism is a theory for a cultural world that to him is disjointed and unlikely: "If there is an Afrofuturism, it must be sought in unlikely places, constellated from far-flung points" (1993, 182). In 2017, as the Black Lives Matter movement advance, and white allies and accomplices examine our psychology to eradicate our own hidden racism that a white supremacist society teaches, these 1993 writings from a white cultural critic look like they stem from a divide and conquer narrative. It is for these reasons that I, and many other ethnographic scholars, advocate prioritizing local cultural ideologies in academic and journalistic analysis.

Afrofuturism essentializes Blackness; Mark Dery's early words and ideas display this ideological tenet, and much of the scholarship that engages Afrofuturism does not challenge it. Afrofuturism assumes a singular, monolithic concept of Blackness that can be applied theoretically to any cultural production whose many varied characteristics include a nod toward the future and Black identity. In a city that has been more than 80 percent Black for more than a century, in a country with other majority Black cities but none near 80 percent, Detroit presents a unique case for site specific study and analysis, in any field or discipline, in African American, African Diasporic, and Black life. I claim that my research does not mix well with Afrofuturism because Afrofuturism does not offer Black liberation, it offers a different, unknown Black future. Detroit techno and house artists, although concerned with futuristic technology, prioritize a utopian world accessible in the music now, in the present. Afrofuturism is not based on collections of facts about Black culture, expressed and framed by Black people; it is not based on ethnographic study centered around first-person narratives and primary sources of Black culture. Afrofuturism scholarship forms its analytical framework around small collections of singular musical, artistic expressions, and applies this framework to a global African Diasporic cultural perspective without suggesting or exploring possible impact on local cultural differences. If Detroit does not fit this framework, then other Black cultural centers and performance styles potentially do not fit the framework, and embracing ideological distinctions that are Black and geographically specific could strengthen any research in Black/African Diasporic studies.

Afrofuturism carries the potential to erase uniqueness and difference in African diasporic existence around the globe. Of Afrofuturism's broad reach, African American literature scholar Daylanne English states, "We define Afrofuturism as African American cultural production and political theory that imagine less constrained black subjectivity in the future and that produce a profound critique of current social, racial, and economic orders" (2013, 217). English, also white, presents Afrofuturism as the primary and most reliable theory for Black cultural analysis and representation, and, at the same time, relies on a "less constrained black subjectivity" as the ultimate future goal, but only for African Americans, not other Black people participating in Black culture around the globe. As English's ideas demonstrate, Afrofuturism does not offer revolution; rather it looks to the future at some point in time and tells Black people to keep waiting, not for Black liberation, but for "less constrained black subjectivity." Black utopianism and safety that waits for no future may look like Black supremacy; however, when compared to centuries of white supremacy, Black utopianism and liberation may simply be balance. Black utopianism that waits for no future may actually, finally, be emancipation and abolition. Seeking utopia and self-sufficiency, Detroit artists and musicians create revolutionary art. Isolation, strength for struggle, rich music and culture, machinery intelligence, and a framework of independence and freedom that even seems to bleed into municipal government structures make Detroit a unique site for protest and change.

Conclusion: Intersectionality and Detroit's Queerphobia

Detroit's stories of musical self-sufficiency, independence, and cultural nationalism display a major weakness: they do not address gender issues or queerphobia. They are not oppressively patriarchal, but they are also not feminist, queer, or transgender affirming. As Black Lives Matter develops further into local chapters and social engagement, Detroit residents continue to mobilize toward community activism, and electronic music culture must answer this intersectional call for political change. Women of color are at the forefront of the Black Lives Matter movement, in person, activity, and ideology, and any work toward Black liberation must embrace all identities.[17] Black Lives Matter leaders state in their guiding principles, "We are committed to building a Black-women affirming space free from sexism, misogyny, and male-centeredness" (Black Lives Matter 2017). In order to be unapologetically Black, those in the service of Black Lives Matter must also be woman-, transgender-, and queer-affirming participants in the movement:

> We are committed to embracing and making space for trans brothers and sisters to participate and lead. We are committed to being self-reflexive and doing the work required to dismantle cis-gender privilege and uplift Black trans folk, especially Black trans women who continue to be disproportionately impacted by trans-antagonistic violence.
>
> We are committed to fostering a queer-affirming network. When we gather, we do so with the intention of freeing ourselves from the tight grip of heteronormative thinking or, rather, the belief that all in the world are heterosexual unless s/he or they disclose otherwise. (Black Lives Matter 2017)

Being unapologetically Black means embracing being unapologetically intersectional, that is, Black and woman, Black and transgender, Black and queer. Detroit suffers from homophobia and transphobia, as does the entire world population. This adversely affects intersectionality of diverse identities in Detroit techno and house music culture because it continues to be a fear-based, exclusionary culture.

Issues of intersectionality must be addressed and included in any cultural, social action dedicated to upholding the guidelines of the Black Lives Matter movement: a movement "guided by the fact that all Black lives [matter], regardless of actual or perceived sexual identity, gender identity, gender expression, economic status, ability, disability, religious beliefs or disbeliefs, immigration status or location" (Black Lives Matter 2017). Electronic music culture and dance club culture begin with a queer history at a global level in which African American DJs contribute much of the cultural and musical innovations, both in Detroit and outside. Larry Levan in New York City, Frankie Knuckles in Chicago, Ken Collier and Stacey Hale in Detroit: these are key historical figures in mid- to late 1970s electronic music culture. Self-identifying as gay, lesbian, and/or queer, these four African American DJs are cornerstones in contemporary dance music culture. Given that the history of queer club culture overlaps and parallels the histories of DJ culture around the United States in the 1970s, it seems timely that organizations like the Detroit Sound Conservancy (DSC) are contributing significant educational and conservation work to linking these histories. The DSC cohosted an event titled "Shoot to Thrill" with the Museum of Contemporary Art Detroit on May 25, 2017. A Detroit techno pioneer, Derrick May, took the stage with the legendary Detroit DJ Greg Collier and others from Detroit's music and art scenes. They shared photographs and told histories, documenting primarily Black queer club culture in Detroit from the 1970s, 1980s, 1990s, and 2000s. Carleton Gholz, a writer and activist, and DSC founder, documents this history in Detroit, explaining that it was first at the gay dance club nights at venues like the Chess Mate, Heaven, and Todd's, where dancers could hear "regular, continuous mixing of prerecorded music" in the mid-1970s (2011, 87).

Established Black DJs and electronic musicians are initiating a resurgence of party spaces and events that are potentially less centered around sexuality as a divisive indicator (traditional options being gay clubs, or clubs where queer sexuality is policed) and more about musical engagement, fashion, communication, and dancing. Dismantling white supremacy while upholding sexism and queerphobia is an impossibility. The global network of oppression that enables white cis-gendered hetero-presenting men to escape and run free also keeps everyone else under constraints. Racism will continue to keep people down if sexism and queer phobia also continue to keep people down. Detroit's small population relative to its land size, paired with its major contributions to music around the globe, makes it a unique microcosm for social change. It feels like a global city while still operating like a small hometown: a hometown crippled by institutionalized patriarchy and white supremacy whose families have to fight for safe public education, basic social services, and healthy food.

Until artists and art scenes do a better job of focusing on intersectionality, Detroit remains a vibrant space for Black Lives Matter activism to flourish at all levels of community engagement. Social activism in Detroit is focused on changing the present, not the future, for African American residents and residents of color. New Era Detroit is one organization "formed to bring back Black unity within growing Black communities. Our focus is empowering and encouraging Black residents in the city of Detroit and around the world to buy, build, invest, and get involved in the communities that they live in" (New Era Detroit 2014). At 82.7 percent African American, the city's activism provides many safe spaces for people of color, and activist organizations protect this type of community engagement, sometimes maintaining Black and Brown membership and not welcoming white people. White activists are allowed to help in other ways outside the boundaries of these

Black safe spaces. Black techno and house musicians contribute entrepreneurial and cultural Black nationalist consciousness to the creation and development of safe/safer spaces for people of color, alongside the social work of organizations like New Era Detroit. Anyone can consume Detroit techno and house music; white people can visit Submerge. However, the message in this musical culture is one of Black liberation via artistic and economic independence. This type of insulated safety in music is essential to Black Lives Matter and any action toward ending white supremacy. White supremacy has for centuries enforced safe, comfortable spaces for white people around the world that exclude and punish people of color. Detroit musicians, artists, and other activists demand, claim, and reestablish safe spaces for people of color with powerful musical mythologies and cultural contributions that threaten to dismantle white supremacy while uplifting Black Lives Matter in movement, philosophy, and action.

NOTES

1. Wachal (2000), 364–365. Stating that Black is synonymous with African American, the linguist Robert S. Wachal insists that *The Chicago Manual of Style* should capitalize Black as a proper noun when referring to Black Americans. I follow this practice. However, white remains lowercase because white does not refer to a culturally and ethnically defined group of people. White denotes various versions of peach-colored skin, but it does not communicate a shared history or cultural background. Black communicates a shared history of human trafficking and enslavement around the globe over centuries. Wachal develops this statement further by explaining that to capitalize African American and not Black is an act of racism.

2. Theo Parrish and his record company, Sound Signature, curated and hosted this Black dance party in northeast Detroit. It was to be a safe space with homemade food and no cameras on the dance floor, and excellent dance music played by Theo Parrish and DJs selected by Parrish.

3. The website http://blacklivesmatter.com cites BYP100 as the originators of the phrase "unapologetically Black." Their mission: "Black Youth Project 100 (BYP100) is an activist member-based organization of Black 18- to 35-year-olds, dedicated to creating justice and freedom for all Black people. We do this through building a network focused on transformative leadership development, non-violent direct action organizing, advocacy and education using a Black queer feminist lens" (Black Youth Project BYP100 2017).

4. A Number of Names (1981); Cybotron (1981).

5. Regarding the use of Latinx, "The 'x' makes Latino, a masculine identifier, gender-neutral. It also moves beyond Latin@—which has been used in the past to include both masculine and feminine identities—to encompass genders outside of that limiting

man-woman binary. Latinx, pronounced 'La-teen-ex,' includes the numerous people of Latin American descent whose gender identities fluctuate along different points of the spectrum, from agender or nonbinary to gender non-conforming, genderqueer and genderfluid" (Reichard 2015).

6. *Roots of Techno: Black DJs and the Detroit Scene*, invited conference, Indiana University, Bloomington, Indiana, October 21, 2006.

7. Regarding police services, it is becoming commonplace and expected to hear people in Detroit's music communities across genre state that they will not call the police.

8. 3.11 refers to March 11, 2011, the date of "the triple disaster of the earthquake, tsunami, and nuclear accident" at Fukushima (Manabe 2015, 3).

9. I did not attend this party and, unfortunately, do not have ethnographic observations to provide.

10. Submerge Underground Railroad, mail-order publication.

11. Motown is, of course, not part of Detroit's underground electronic music and dance club culture, but the influence of Motown artists and history is prominent and celebrated in local DJ culture.

12. Moodymann 1997. The liner notes are printed without capital letters except for KDJ (Kenny Dixon Jr.). The "N" word is present in this quote because that is how it appears in Moodymann's liner notes. It would be presumptuous of me to change the wording because this statement is in his voice, not mine.

13. An LP, or album, contains multiple songs—usually more than two—on each side. An EP, or extended-play record, holds about two to four songs on each side, sometimes different songs, or different versions of the same song. It can be a 7-inch, 10-inch, or 12-inch record playing at 33 1/3, 45, or 78 rpm. A 12-inch is one type of EP record; it holds one or two songs on each side. A DJ typically plays 12-inch EPs because allowing a single piece of music to stretch out in the grooves spinning around an EP record produces a much louder, fuller sound in contrast to the sound produced from four, five, or six songs taking up that same amount of space on an LP.

14. *Aquatic Invasion* (1995), Underground Resistance, EP; *Molecular Enhancement* (1994), Rephlex, EP; *Digital Tsunami* (2001), Tresor, EP; *Neptune's Lair* (1999), Tresor, LP; "Wavejumper" (1995), *Aquatic Invasion*, Underground Resistance, EP; "Bubble Metropolis" (1993), *Bubble Metropolis*, Underground Resistance, EP.

15. Drexciya, *Grava 4* (2002), Clone LP.

16. Rubin, Mike. 2017. "Infinite Journey to Inner Space: The Legacy of Drexciya." June 29, 2017. Red Bull Music Academy. http://daily.redbullmusicacademy.com/2017/06/drexciya-infinite-journey-to-inner-space.

17. The founders of Black Lives Matter are three Black women: Opal Tometi, Alicia Garza, and Patrisse Cullors.

DISCOGRAPHY

Cybotron. 1981. *Alleys of Your Mind*. Deep Space Records. 107043X. Vinyl 7-inch.
Drexciya. 1992. *Deep Sea Dweller*. Shockwave Records. SW1007. Vinyl 12-inch.

———. 1993. *Drexciya 2—Bubble Metropolis*. Underground Resistance. UR-026. Vinyl 12-inch.

———. 1994. *Drexciya 3—Molecular Enhancement*. Rephlex. 017. Vinyl 12-inch.

———. 1995. *Aquatic Invasion*. Underground Resistance. UR-030. Vinyl 12-inch.

———. 1997. *The Quest*. Submerge. SVE-7. Vinyl 2×12-inch. Compilation.

———. 1999. *Neptune's Lair*. Tresor. Tresor 129. Vinyl 2×12-inch. LP.

———. 2001. *Digital Tsunami*. Tresor. Tresor 182. Vinyl 12-inch.

———. 2002. *Grava 4*. Clone. C#25. Vinyl 2×12-inch. LP.

Lil Louis. 1987. *Frequency/How I Feel*. Dance Mania. DM 008. Vinyl 12-inch.

Moodymann. 1997. *Silentintroduction*. Planet E. PE65234. Vinyl 2×12-inch. LP.

———. 2001. *J.A.N.* KDJ. KDJ30. Vinyl 12-inch. Single-sided.

———. 2008. *Det.riot '67*. KDJ. KDJ37. Vinyl 2×12-inch. LP.

Rhythim Is Rhythim. 1987. *Strings of Life*. Transmat. MS 004. Vinyl 12-inch.

A Number of Names. 1981. *Sharevari*. Capriccio Records. P-928. Vinyl 12-inch.

VIDEOGRAPHY

Bredow, Gary, director. 2006. *High Tech Soul: The Creation of Techno Music*. Plexifilm. DVD.

INTERVIEWS

Brendan M. Gillen. Interview with author, July 22, 2009.

Todd Osborn. Interview with author, September 12, 2008.

Aaron Siegel. Interview with author, February 5, 2011.

WORKS CITED

Black Lives Matter. 2017. https://blacklivesmatter.com/about/what-we-believe/. Accessed February 9, 2017.

Black Youth Project BYP100. 2017. https://blackyouthproject.com/byp100-launches-unapologetically-black-t-shirt-campaign/. Accessed February 25, 2017.

David, Marlo. 2007. "Afrofuturism and Post-Soul Possibility in Black Popular Music." *African American Review* 41, no. 4, Post-Soul Aesthetic (Winter, 2007): 695–707.

Dery, Mark. 1993. "Black to the Future: Interviews with Samuel R. Delany, Greg Tate, and Tricia Rose." In *Flame Wars: The Discourse of Cyberculture*, edited by Mark Dery, 179–222. Durham, NC: Duke University Press.

English, Daylanne and Alvin Kim. 2013. "Now We Want Our Funk Cut: Janelle Monáe's Neo-Afrofuturism." American Studies, 52 (4): 217–230.

Eshun, Kodwo. 2003. "Further Considerations on Afrofuturism." *CR: The New Centennial Review* 3, no. 2 (Summer): 287–302.

Fikentscher, Kai. 2000. *"You Better Work!" Underground Dance Music in New York City*. Hanover, NH: University Press of New England.

Fisher, Mark. 2007. "Mike Banks Interview, Unedited Transcript." *The Wire,* November 2007. https://www.thewire.co.uk/in-writing/interviews/mike-banks-interview.

Gholz, Carleton. 2011. "'Where the Mix Is Perfect': Voices from the Post-Motown Soundscape." PhD diss., University of Pittsburgh.

Manabe, Noriko. 2015. *The Revolution Will Not Be Televised: Protest Music after Fukushima*. New York: Oxford University Press.

Morrison, Toni. 2015. "No Place for Self-Pity, No Room for Fear: In Times of Dread, Artists Must Never Choose to Remain Silent." *The Nation*, March 23, 2015: 184–185.

New Era Detroit. 2014. Mission Statement. http://neweradetroit.com/about/missionstatement/

Reichard, Raquel. 2015. "Why We Say Latinx: Trans and Gender Non-Conforming People Explain." *Latina*, August 29, 2015. http://www.latina.com/lifestyle/our-issues/why-we-say-latinx-trans-gender-non-conforming-people-explain.

Sicko, Dan. (1999) 2010. *Techno Rebels: Renegades of Electronic Funk*. 2nd ed. Detroit, MI: Wayne State University Press.

Sound Signature. 2017. "The Mission of Music Gallery and Last Friday's Event." June 2, 2017. http://soundsignature.net/archives/.

Toffler, Alvin. 1970. *Future Shock*. New York: Random House.

———. 1980. *The Third Wave*. New York: Morrow.

US Census Bureau. 2016. QuickFacts: Detroit, Michigan. https://www.census.gov/quickfacts/table/PST045215/2622000/. Accessed December 1, 2016.

Wachal, Robert S. 2000. "The Capitalization of *Black* and *Native American*." *American Speech* 75 (4): 364–365.

Wolffe, Jerry. 2010. "Oakland Plummets on List of Wealthy Counties." *Oakland Press News*, September 9, 2010. http://www.theoaklandpress.com/article/OP/20100924/NEWS/309249882

DENISE DALPHOND is an independent public-sector ethnomusicologist. Her areas of interest are Detroit techno and house music. She writes about music and activism at schoolcraftwax.work.

CONCLUSION: RACE, PLACE, AND PEDAGOGY IN THE BLACK LIVES MATTER ERA

Stephanie Shonekan

BLACK LIVES MATTER AND MUSIC has been concerned with a particular historical moment of racial injustice, struggle, and activism in the United States. Throughout history, there have been similar moments like this because of what Langston Hughes called "dreams deferred." The promise of equality and justice for all, pledged in the Constitution, has never been fully realized. In other countries, forms of injustice are reflected through tribal, religious, class, gender, and language differences. Throughout history, human beings have created hierarchies to establish positions of power and dominance and to create subordinate groups on which to wield this power. For the United States, one of the most enduring factors for the establishment of power has been race, distilled to its most basic definition, the color of the skin. Historically, this artificial construction has had real ramifications, pitting whites against blacks, blacks against browns, light-skinned against dark-skinned. Other factors have featured, so that there are classism, sexism, homophobia, ageism, ableism—but none has remained as long or damaged as deeply as racism. At every juncture, groups of justice-minded Americans have fought back, inscribing a tradition of activism into history books and giving hope to every generation that racism cannot continue as the status quo in a country that has always promised liberty and justice for all.

Over the centuries, these activists have come from different sectors of experience and profession—politicians, visual artists, preachers, train porters, poets, lawyers, athletes, musicians, scholars, and teachers—all ordinary people unwilling to let racial injustice go unchecked. The Black Lives Matter movement has served this generation's need to agitate against the institution of systemic racism, which is a fundamental threat to not only blacks in America, but everybody in America. Whether at the center of the movement or on the periphery, those involved with holding America accountable to the notion that black lives have always been in jeopardy include all the sectors of Americans that participated in earlier movements for civil rights. There is a sense of responsibility that reminds us that hope is only viable when it is nurtured and tended. When this is done, hope is tangible and change seems possible.

The group of us who came together to write this book are among the scores of Americans who think it is important to focus on the ways in which the United States is changing in terms of racial justice. As scholars, all trained at Indiana University's Department of Folklore and Ethnomusicology, we have a special calling to consider the life and work of the folk, in this case, the American folk. Beyond that, we were all moved and personally involved in discourses and real-life experiences where race is a serious matter. We were taught to think critically about the narratives that we tell each other about the world we live in, whether these are in stories, art, material culture, or songs. The intertwined fields of folklore and ethnomusicology offer us a means of engaging with the different traditions and expressions of the folk.

Black Lives Matter and Music has been about the music soundscape and the musical communities that surround this particular moment in US race relations with a specific focus on place and pedagogy. From the first gathering we arranged at the Society for Ethnomusicology conference to the American Folklore Society conference the following year, we were mostly concerned with how we might help expound on the Black Lives Matter movement; that is, how we teach, how we conduct research, and, ultimately, how we should think about this current historical moment and this particular space. Concentrating on this time and place does not negate the need to expand the focus, as we are aware of the far-reaching ripples of effect that this movement has had around the world, such as the #FeesMustFall campaign in South Africa and other acts of solidarity in Canada, Nigeria, and elsewhere. In *Freedom Is a Constant Struggle*, the activist and scholar Angela Davis observes, "Ferguson reminds us that we need to globalize our thinking about these issues" (2016, 13), and this project should be viewed as a step toward conducting research in other areas of the world where work is being done by scholars and activists in different fields and disciplines.

Our particular focus on place, with five chapters capturing the stories and musical cultures of distinct cities—Columbia, Missouri; Bloomington, Indiana; Detroit, Michigan; Washington, DC; and Houston, Texas—is important because it serves to remind us of the diversity within the American landscape. These chapters offer nuanced snapshots of how African American genres have flourished in different cities and the current movement's effect on its population. The other two chapters focus on a different kind of space, the American campus, but also shift the focus to pedagogy, challenging readers to think of how activism and social justice work might appear in the American higher education classroom. As I reflect on the mission of Black Studies, I often straddle that pedagogical line that separates teaching scholarship from teaching activism. As students become more involved in activism themselves, we have to assess how to buoy them with the historical context and framework to help them think critically about their world. For instance, recognizing that the Mizzou events were triggered by the N-word, I decided to develop a new course about just that. Part of the description for the proposed course is as follows:

> One of the most loaded and problematic words in US cultural history is "Nigger." The articulation of the word has often been the trigger for extreme racial tension at different times and in different parts of the country, including our Mizzou campus. It is disturbing that in a so-called, post-racial America, this term, with its deep roots in slavery, is still used with the purpose of demeaning African Americans. Interestingly, throughout the 1970s and by the 1990s, the word was "reclaimed," repurposed, and redefined as "nigga" by young African Americans, the vibrant and influential hip hop generation. Thus, a variant of the word was employed in vernacular and in hip hop lyrics. That seemed to indicate to some members of the mainstream audience, one of the largest groups to purchase hip hop music, that the word could be utilized by all. However, the six-letter word and its variant, have become cultural signifiers that connote everything from hatred to camaraderie, with inherent rules and parameters for who can use them and what they ultimately mean. This course will trace the etymology of the word from its early iterations as "nigger" in literature and memoir, to its evolution as it branches off to "nigga" in hip hop. We will study

key texts and albums with a view to understanding and peeling back the various layers that have preserved this word as a critical signifier of Black identity in the US and beyond.

Other teachers have adjusted their portfolio of courses to include new courses that address topics of significant social and cultural impact. As instructors, it is our duty to create new and innovative curricula to help our students process the sensitive and real matters that revolve around them in everyday life. Hence, this is the age of critical syllabi that are circulated via social media, such as the #Ferguson syllabus created by Marcia Chatelain and the Black Lives Matter syllabus created by Frank Leon Roberts.

In addition to creating new courses, some professors are adjusting their existing courses to include contemporary social justice issues. For instance, immediately following the murder of Michael Brown, three major tracks were released by black artists: "Don't Shoot" by The Game et al., "Black Rage" by Lauryn Hill, and "Be Free" by J. Cole. Each of these songs was a reaction to the tragic injustice of Brown's murder and a reflection of the sentiment that was so palpable among the urban black community. Although I was teaching a global hip hop class when these songs came out, I decided to offer these three samples to the class for critique. After all, I reasoned, the world is appropriating and customizing US hip hop, and this was an opportunity to study hip hop's return to an important part of its roots, as a purposeful, socially conscious tool for the black community in the United States. Also, these artists model what it is that so many of us are doing, mixing our profession with the urgency of activism. I asked my students to interact on our discussion board, to determine which hip hop/R&B sample was most successful in capturing the issues surrounding the racial tension of 2014–2015.

This assignment was a welcome adjustment to the syllabus, one that brought the real world into our classroom.[1] Students described "Don't Shoot" by The Game as an extensive ode to Brown and Ferguson, with some good storytelling by a diverse group of rappers. One student explained that, of the three, this was "most effective only because of how it sounds. It sounds like the mainstream material that people would turn up to." Agreeing with this view, a student said it was good to hear "so many different artists voicing their opinions and sorrow for this event." In contrast, a student thought "Don't Shoot" to be "a little gimmicky [but] I commend him for the hands-on approach he took by giving back to the Ferguson community." Another student criticized "the children singing the chorus. I also didn't think this song should have been that long for the quality of the beat." Agreeing with this criticism of the length, another student said, "The message kind of got redundant after the first 3 or 4 rappers."

Regarding Lauryn Hill's "Black Rage," a sarcastic play on "My Favorite Things" from *The Sound of Music,* a student reflected that this song "is effective because it does give the sense that [Hill] just had something to say or express, and music was her best outlet. She didn't have to manufacture an entire song, just make sure her emotions were written down as lyrics." Another student commented on her persona, explaining that the song "will get respect just because it's Ms. Lauryn Hill. The arrangement of it reminds us of her style, but it would be too raw for airplay." Another student lauded her: "Ms. Hill's stating of facts, and giving root causes to what we're facing every day all while ironically matching the tone of such a happy song cherished by the oppressors is pure genius." Another student explored Hill's contribution to the movement: "she spoke about the causes of the conditions many Blacks face in their environment. I feel as though this kind of song could be the answer to those who question why there is so much outrage in Black communities."

J. Cole was described by one of the students as "the most conscious rapper in the game as of now." Many of the students concurred, with one describing the melody of "Be Free" as "oozing from his image so it will not be looked down upon and the message is very straight-forward for the younger and older audience." One student described the quality and sincerity of J. Cole's voice: "There is pain, anger, sorrow, and wonder in his voice. J. Cole speaks his truth." Another student revealed that she "thought of this song as one of the soundtracks of the Black Lives Matter movement. The way J. Cole delivers his message matches the tone of what was occurring in Ferguson at this time. His delivery is soulful." Reemphasizing this quality, a student said, "The emotion in [J. Cole's] voice is so moving." Not all the students favored this song. One student said "I think 'Be Free' by J. Cole was the least effective. The lyrics were great and I loved how he incorporated the events into his music, but ... I would have wanted more lyrics in the song." A final comment on J. Cole: "He reaches a more diverse audience than Lauryn Hill or the Game, so I think his song's reach across different races is important too."

At several points in this book we have mentioned Kendrick Lamar's "Alright" as the anthem for the movement. It was important for my students to see that other artists and songs are actively engaged with the movement. We discussed these songs in class and compared them to older civil rights songs like Marvin Gaye's "What's Going On" and Nina Simone's "Mississippi Goddam." Apart from the valuable pedagogical detour that this assignment presented, the content of and context for these songs exemplify what the contributors to this book have attempted to do: my students reflected on and critiqued music that was in response to one particular incident in the city of Ferguson, a unique space where police demographics and attitudes as well as social structure allowed for a combustible environment, that reflected the concerns of the Black Lives Matter movement. We contend that it is these organic pedagogical forays, which many of my colleagues do on a daily basis, that allow us to forge new paths in the humanities, and that will take us to fresh understandings of where we are in history and of who we are as Americans and as human beings. These are the exercises that work as gateways into folkloristic and ethnomusicological discourse, balancing the critique of narratives, the analysis of sonic compositions, and the examination of social and cultural values of artists' communities. It is my hope that such approaches will prepare our students to think critically about how they will contribute to a more just society.

As this current generation of millennial students absorb new knowledge and grapple with what their roles will be in this troubled society, my generation of scholars and instructors—and those that came before us—realize that, as Angela Davis reminds us, this struggle is constant with every new event or tragedy that threatens to push us back from progress. Inevitably embroiled in problematic national politics, our public institutions are often spaces that are precarious for those of us who teach in the humanities and social sciences and who venture into new pedagogical waters. So we too ask ourselves about the character of our roles and the sturdiness of our platforms. The June 2017 edition of *Ebony* magazine features an article on the rapper-activist Chance the Rapper and his album *The Coloring Book* (2016), which represents his preoccupation and passion for collective social justice and personal spiritual growth. The *Ebony* article reveals him as an artist who cares deeply about his Chicago community. He explains: "I fully respect my platform to impact social change" (Gibbs 2017, 80). In this book, we have each been mindful about our scholarly platforms, first nurtured at Indiana University by mentors like Portia Maultsby, who led the way for scholarship on black popular music and culture both in the US and as it sprouts abroad; Ruth Stone, whose work on West African and Middle Eastern music provided a blueprint for understanding how to write about music and lived experiences; Richard Bauman, who taught us to pay careful and particular attention to performance spaces and practices; and Mellonee Burnim, whose focus on African American gospel music inspired us to trace the trajectory of the sacred musical tradition as it evolved in the United States.

Emerging from these mentors, contributors to this book represent an extension of this training by delving into the music and culture of a specific identity and experience with a careful eye on the effect of the Black Lives Matter era. As such, Langston Collin Wilkins considers how the SLAB culture in Houston creates a unique black identity; Denise Dalphond digs into the ways that house music culture celebrates black identity in Detroit; Alison Martin analyzes the impact of go-go music and culture on the black community in DC; and Fernando Orejuela and Stephanie Shonekan concentrate on how this type of work can be dealt with on college campuses. We all hope to inspire our readers to think about how black struggle, liberation, and identity have evolved in the US and around the world, and how folklore and music offer us a ready way of observing, analyzing, and learning.

Notes

1. Thanks to the students who consented to my use of their quotes for this chapter: Stuart Goodwin, Mubinah Khaleel, Kyara Malone, Jessie Martin, Tateanna McCaskill, Kennedy Moore, Diamond Stacker, and Xavier Williams.

Works Cited

Davis, Angela. 2016. *Freedom Is a Constant Struggle: Ferguson, Palestine, and the Foundations of a Movement*. Chicago: Haymarket.

Gibbs, Adrienne Samuels. 2017. "Chance the Rapper for President." *Ebony* (June): 79–84.

STEPHANIE SHONEKAN is Associate Professor of Ethnomusicology and Black Studies at the University of Missouri. She is author of *Soul, Country and the USA: Race and Identity in American Music* and *The Life of Camilla Williams, African American Classical Singer and Opera Diva*.

INDEX

Bauman, Richard, 6, 44, 117; *A World of Others' Words*, 45–46
Beyoncé: "Freedom," 70, 81; *Lemonade*, 28; "No Angel" (2013), 66
Big Mello, "Wegonefunkwichamind" (1994), 60
Black Atlantean mythology. *See* Drexciya: Drexciyan sea narrative
Black Codes, 80
black experience: and emotional justice, 71–72; of Houston, 59, 61–63, 68; learning through hip hop culture, 52; and musical culture, 38; music as window into, xii; of systematic oppression and dehumanization, 67. *See also* racism
Black Hippy (West Coast), 51
black liberation movements, music in, 15, 21. *See also* black musical communities and culture in Detroit
Black Lives Matter movement: anthems of, 1; belief in narrated texts, 47; criticism of, xi–xii, 73–74, 78–79, 83n4; description of, ix, 7; ideals, objectives, and activities of, xi, 67–68, 70–71, 73, 87, 104–5, 112; inclusiveness of, 68; music released in tandem with, 2–3, 11n2; partnering organizations, 49; start of, 2, 72; use of music in, xi. *See also* black musical communities and culture in Detroit; go-go music and culture in Washington, DC; Mizzou movement; racial inequality, teaching about through hip hop; SLAB culture
black musical communities and culture in Detroit, 86–108; evolution of electronic music culture, 89–92; musical mythology of, 97–104; overview of, 86–89; protest in Detroit's dance culture and techno music, 92–97; queerphobia and intersectionality in, 104–7
black music as lens to understand black life, 32
"Black Music Matters: Taking Stock" (roundtable), 2–4
black nationalism, 40, 86, 87, 92, 96, 97–98
blackness, Afrofuturism concept of, 102, 103

Black Panthers, 19, 40–41
Black Power, xi, 5, 7, 15
Blackwell, Michelle, 77
Bland, Sandra, 81
Bloc Boyz Click, 64; "Officially Ridin' Swings" (music video), 61
Bloomington (Indiana). *See* Indiana University; racial inequality, teaching about through hip hop
blues music, 30
Blunt, Corey, 60
Bohlman, Philip, 71
Bonnette, Lakeyta M., *Pulse of the People*, 50–51
Booze Traveler (TV show), 66
Botkin, Benjamin A., 5
bounce beat, 76, 83n7
Brown, Michael, 2, 114
Browne, Simone, *Dark Matters* (2015), 79–80
Buchanan, John, 78
Burnim, Mellonee, 5, 11n3, 21, 76, 117
Butler, Jonathan, 3, 17–18, 19, 24

Cadillac cars, 56, 59
campus racism. *See* Mizzou movement; racial inequality, teaching about through hip hop
"candy paint," 58
Carlos, John, 22
Castile, Philando, 7, 10, 70, 83n1
Chance the Rapper, *The Coloring Book*, 28, 116
chants, use of, 19
Chatelain, Marcia, 114
choral singing, improvisational, 1
Chuck Brown and the Soul Searchers, 75, 78
civil rights movement, ix, 4, 5, 7, 15, 18–19, 74–75, 112, 116
C-Note, 60
Cole, J., "Be Free" (2014), 2, 114, 115
Collier, Greg, 106
Collier, Ken, 105
Columbia (Missouri). *See* Mizzou movement

CPSIA information can be obtained
at www.ICGtesting.com
Printed in the USA
LVHW071718170119
604287LV00024B/382/P